150 Key Concepts in
philosophy

contradiction

agency

empathy

knowledge

morality

What's the Difference?

ethics   belief

sympathy

power

paradox

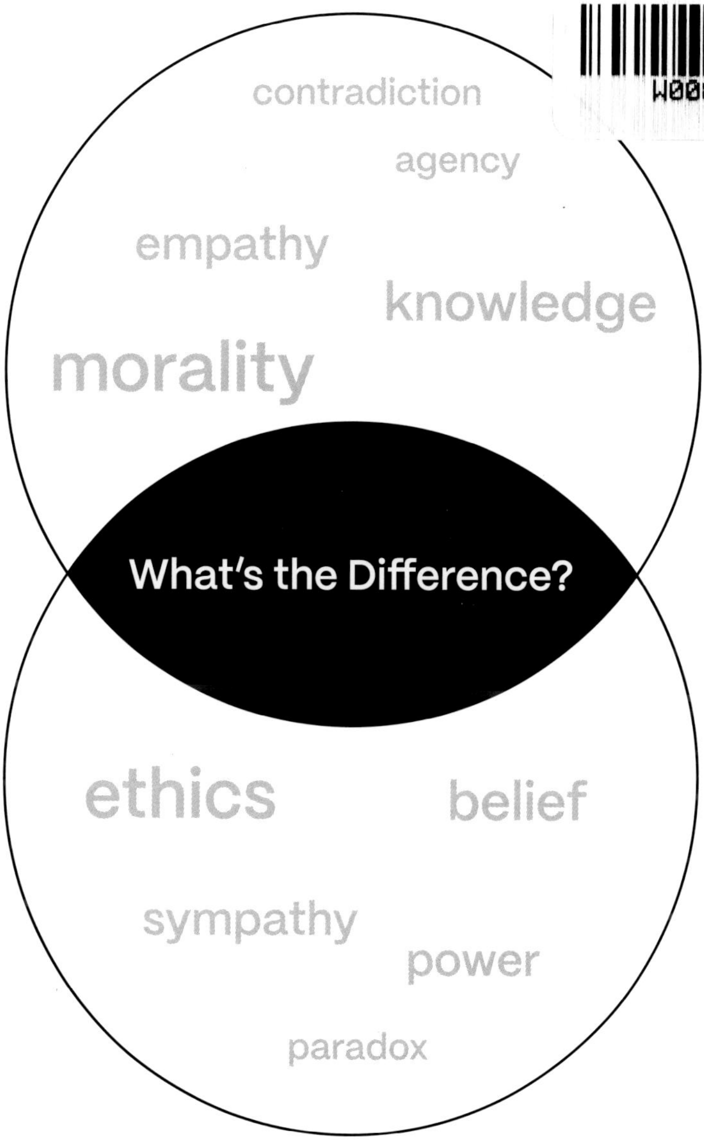

IVY PRESS

introduction

This book is part of a new series and a brand-new approach to popular reference based on the question, 'What's the difference?'. Inside, there are crystal-clear explanations of 150 paired words that build into a comprehensive philosophy primer. Philosophical concepts are explored in pairs to help clarify common (and not so common) confusions. Exploring two definitions at the same time cuts to the heart of a topic quickly and clearly and helps avoid those all too frequent conceptual slip-ups. If you're worried about mistaking 'aesthetic' and 'ascetic', confusing 'implication' and 'inference', then this is the book for you.

What's the Difference: Philosophy explains 150 key philosophical topics in engaging and easy to understand ways, covering big ticket topics such as epistemology (the study of knowledge), aesthetics (the study of art) and metaphysics (the study of reality itself!) The first of the three sections is focused on everyday mix-ups. When you say something's 'false', is that the same as saying it's 'wrong'? What about 'right' and 'true'? These are words that we use on a daily basis. Their meanings sometimes overlap, but the distinctions are important – especially if you want to tell the difference between right and wrong ... or should that be true and false?

The second section examines slightly more technical terms, focusing on concepts like 'paradox' and 'contradiction'. These are ideas a lot of us are familiar with, but occasionally misuse. If we're not precise in how we use these words, we risk talking past each other and ending up in conversational cul-de-sacs.

The final section of the book looks at those finnicky, but crucial distinctions between philosophical terms such as 'animism' and 'animalism'. This section not only clarifies distinctions, it will also extend your conceptual vocabulary. Whether you're interested in the everyday, the technical or the esoteric, there's something in here for everyone – beginner, student and practitioner alike.

In addition to metaphysics, epistemology and aesthetics, you'll find discussions of political philosophy (what's the difference between 'autocracy' and 'totalitarianism'?) and morality (or should that be ethics?) There are several entries on formal logic (the study of arguments) as well as the philosophy of science ('scientific' or 'scientistic'?), the philosophy of race (what's the difference between 'privilege' and 'power') and the philosophy of humour.

If you want to know the difference between emotions and moods, sarcasm and irony, sex and gender, then read on. This book will help make the difference between a chatterbox and a brainbox, a sophist and a sage, and a well-informed argument and a sloppy debate.

how to use this book

Each double-page spread is designed to make the concepts clear and accessible. Expert text explains each key term, from the basic idea to the nuanced concept.

---

equality

Equality refers to the state of being equal. No surprises there. Most of the time, when you hear it mentioned, it's in relation to political and legal rights. If you support gender equality, for example, you support the idea that all individuals, regardless of their gender, should have the same fundamental legal rights and access to resources.

Within sexist societies (which, let's be honest, are most societies), men and women and non-binary folk are treated differently. Within patriarchies (from the Greek, *patria-arche*, meaning 'rule of the father'), the imbalance overtly favours men. If you're a man, you are statistically more likely to get a better paid job than women and non-binary people who are similarly qualified. This is an unequal situation grounded in the perceived superiority of men.

It is only in the past few decades that some governments have attempted to address the disparities that occur in law. For example, it was after the 1975 Sex Discrimination Act was passed in the UK that women were allowed to apply for mortgages, and in 2010 that the Equality Act addressed the legal neglect of sexual harassment of women at work and in public. In 2017 it became mandatory for workplaces to report the disparities in pay between male and female employees (the so-called 'gender pay gap').

However, achieving equality does not necessarily mean treating everyone exactly the same (equally), because different individuals or groups may require different measures to address existing disparities. This leads us to the concept of equity ...

 In a nutshell
The state of being equal.

Why it matters
It is an important political goal to provide the same (equal) rights and resources to everyone, regardless of their background.

Key figures
Simone de Beauvoir, 1908–1986
Anna Julia Cooper, 1858–1964
Karl Marx, 1818–1883
Paul C. Taylor, b.1967
Sojourner Truth, c.1797–1883

Make the connection
liberalism, p.47
sexism, p.48
oppression, p.52
identity politics, p.90

equity

Since people are born into different situations, equal treatment can only really be provided if resources are distributed based on individual needs. Treating people *equally* requires treating them the same (i.e., giving them the same resources). Treating people *equitably* means that resources may be allocated in a way that appears unequal. Some people, who have been disadvantaged by society, are due more than others.

Equitable treatment recognizes and attempts to rectify historical and systemic disadvantages. The aim is to provide everyone with a genuine opportunity to succeed, irrespective of their identity or their socio-economic background. Imagine a group of people trying to watch a football match over a wall. We want them all to see the game. Treating them equally, we would give them boxes of the same size to stand on, regardless of their height. This wouldn't necessarily help the shortest among them, who need larger boxes than taller people. By contrast, if we wanted to treat them equitably we would give each person a box relative in size to their height: children would have larger boxes; tall people and people wearing 1970s-style platform shoes would have smaller ones.

Equality focuses on sameness. Everyone is entitled to the same legal protections, the same access to resources, the same work opportunities. Equity emphasizes fairness and justice over sameness, and equitable treatment is treatment that acknowledges pre-existing disparities, addressing them differently in order to ensure everyone has an opportunity to succeed.

In a nutshell
Equitable treatment takes advantages and disadvantages into account in order to level a playing field.

Why it matters
Equal treatment doesn't always solve social inequality. Our policies need to be responsive to pre-existing conditions.

Key figures
Moya Bailey
Kimberlé Crenshaw, b.1959
Peggy McIntosh, b.1934
Charles W. Mills, 1951–2021

Make the connection
power, p.41
racism, p.51
prescriptive, p.74
communism, p.92

In a nutshell is a single-sentence summary of each concept.

Why it matters gives the context for how the concept relates to our day-to-day lives.

Key figures names those all-important folk engaged in the debate.

Make the connection helps to navigate connections across the book.

5

The illustrations offer a visual way to understand tricky ideas.

identity

'I'm Adam and I'm a writer. I wrote this book. I'm also a Libra, a twin, and I'm Jewish and, at the time of writing this sentence, I have a big beard with a few flecks of grey in it.'

These few sentences describe different elements of someone's identity (my identity). This is how we normally use the word 'identity': to refer to a person's character, background, heritage and facts about them. When we're talking about identity, we're usually talking about things that are important to one's sense of self – the things that make me *me* and you *you*.

There are items on the list above that aren't *essential* to me, Adam, but they're still important. People aren't born writers. They become them and can cease to be them too. I can certainly stop having a beard (it's the work of a few minutes). Similarly, being a person sitting on the bus is not, I would say, part of my identity, even if it's a true description for short periods of time.

Some aspects of our identities are beyond our control. I can't help the fact that I'm a Libra; that's just a way to describe the fact that I was born in a certain month. If you think of Jewishness as an ethnicity, then I can't stop being Jewish either. Importantly, however, these things can be subject to social policies (e.g., laws). Our identities are deeply personal, but also the focus of political action. In some countries, there are laws that protect people from discrimination based on their identity.

In a nutshell
Refers to character, heritage or personhood.

Why it matters
Your identity is, by definition, that which makes you special and different from everyone else. Even identical twins don't have the same identity.

Key figures
Talia Mae Bettcher
Judith Butler, b.1956
Kimberlé Crenshaw, b.1959
Audre Lorde, 1934–1992

Make the connection

I'm a writer!

identity

In formal logic, 'identity' means something slightly different to character or personhood. Identity is represented by the equals symbol (=) and refers to a logical relation of *being the same*. If we say, for instance, that Mary Anne Evans is identical to George Eliot, we're claiming that they're the same person.

The logic of identity has been much puzzled over. Most people interested in identity agree that it has certain special features. For one thing, it's a symmetrical relation. If Mary Anne Evans is identical to George Eliot, then the same is true in reverse. Identity is also transitive, which is to say it travels. If Mary is identical to George and George is identical to the author of *Middlemarch*, then Mary is identical to the author of *Middlemarch*. So-called 'identicals' are also indiscernible, which is to say that if this thing is identical to that thing, then any property the former has, the latter has too – and vice versa.

It's relatively easy to distinguish between the different uses of identity. Matters become more complicated when we enter the metaphysical subfield known as 'personal identity', where the focus is the identity of identities, as it were. The central question is: What makes this person the *same* person over time? The person reading these words right now is the same person (i.e., is identical with) a certain baby born on a certain day. But *why*? What is it that makes you identical to that baby?

In a nutshell
The logical relation of sameness, represented by the equals symbol.

Why it matters
The concept of identity is essential to logic, mathematics and, indeed, our everyday navigation of the world.

Key figures
Gottfried Wilhelm Liebniz, 1646–1716
John Locke, 1632–1704
Lynne Rudder Baker, 1944–2017
David Wiggins, b.1933

Make the connection

Are we all the same?

knowledge

I know the earth is roughly spheroid. I also know that my name is Adam and (unrelatedly), that 2 + 2 = 4. Or at least I *think* I know these things. How do I know that I know them? Answers to this age-old philosophical question depend on what we take knowledge to be. In one, now classic formulation, my use of the verb 'to know' is accurate if these statements are grounded in justified true belief.

Take, for instance, the shape of the earth. Most of us genuinely believe our planet is roughly spheroid. We're not pretending to think this. Moreover, the belief is justified. I realize I don't have any direct experience of the world being spheroid (I've never been off-planet and seen it from a distance), but reputable scientific authorities have, for a long time, provided compelling evidence to support this view.

Is it true, though? This is trickier. For my belief to be true, it needs to correspond to reality. It must actually, factually be the case that the earth is roughly spheroid, irrespective of what people think and scientists say. This is where philosophers – particularly those interested in epistemology, the study of knowledge – can begin to lose their grip. Hallucinations and virtual reality cause us to question the reliability of our access to the external world. Maybe the external world is flat. Maybe it's a cube. Maybe it doesn't exist at all.

In a nutshell
According to some, knowledge is justified true belief.

Why it matters
Our ability to distinguish knowledge from false beliefs (or even true beliefs) allows us to make rational decisions in a world full of misinformation and fake news.

Key figures
Nancy Cartwright, b.1944
René Descartes, 1596–1650
Kristie Dotson, b.1975
Edmund L. Gettier, 1927–2021

Make the connection
rationality, p.14
scepticism, p.56
existence, p.70
subjective, p.76

belief

Epistemologists can get caught up on the question of reality. 'Am I dreaming?!' they cry. 'Is this all a computer simulation!?' Most of us, however, go about our business without worrying too much about the existence of the external world. We're not especially concerned about the metaphysical pitfalls of saying we 'know' this or that. Perhaps we're simply claiming that we believe it, just really robustly.

Beliefs are themselves worth investigation. Some are more fragile than others. We may say, tentatively, that we believe something has happened when it's there, on the cusp of memory, and we can't quite recall the details. (Do you remember your seventh birthday? Kind of?) Other beliefs, like those grounded in (seemingly) reliable data or vivid experience, appear to be sturdier. Did I just have a toasted bagel for lunch? Yes, there are still crumbs on my sweater. Do I *know* that I just had a toasted bagel for lunch? Given the (incredibly unlikely) possibility that I've experienced some sort of hallucination, I can't say for sure, so I am only really licensed to say I *believe* so – but I believe very strongly.

The difference between knowledge and belief is that the former has to be ratified by reality – it needs to be *true* – whereas the latter is less dependent on the external world. Some philosophers, particularly theologians, emphasize the distinctive virtues of belief. This can be a sign of intellectual humility, a recognition that some things (maybe many) lie beyond the ambit of human perception.

In a nutshell
Belief can be a sign of intellectual humility and a deference to a higher authority.

Why it matters
Belief – and faith – require interpersonal trust, dependence and a secure attachment to others.

Key figures
Teresa of Ávila, 1515–1582
Augustine of Hippo, c.354–430 CE
Kate Manne, b.1983
Julian of Norwich c.1342–1416

Make the connection
phenomenology, p.118
agnostic, p.139
solipsism, p.143

I believe the moon is made of cheese.

imply

If it's raining, then the ground will be wet. It's a relatively banal statement, isn't it? Unfortunately, if there's one thing philosophers like to do with banal statements, it's make them more complicated. For logicians – philosophers interested in the structure and validity of arguments – statements like this are comprised of two parts. The first is the 'antecedent' (it's raining), the second is the 'consequent' (the ground will be wet); the second follows, i.e. is *implied by*, the first. 'Implication' refers to the relationship between two propositions. In formal logic, this relationship is represented by the arrow symbol (→) and captured by the phrasing 'If ... then ...'

When we talk about implication, we're not necessarily talking about causation. It's true that the rain *might* cause the ground to get wet, but there are plenty of reasons for the ground to be wet that have nothing to do with the rain. Maybe a water main has burst? And even if it's raining, the ground can remain dry (under a bus shelter or a gazebo). Implication describes a correlation, not causation.

The logic of implication allows us to hint at something without actually saying it. 'Those diamond cufflinks look *remarkably* similar to the ones stolen from the marquis last week.' Hearing this, you might well think that the cufflinks in question are *in fact* the ones stolen from the marquis last week – *if* they are identical, *then* they are the stolen cufflinks (though, again, the fact that they are identical doesn't cause them to be stolen).

In a nutshell
Implication is a logical relation between two propositions: an antecedent, which entails a consequent.

Why it matters
Understanding implication is central to our ability to comprehend, and converse with, each other (without spelling everything out).

Key figures
G. E. M. Anscombe, 1919–2001
Dorothy Edgington, b.1941
Hilary Putnam, 1926–2016
Gillian Russell

Make the connection

infer

People sometimes use 'infer' as a synonym for 'imply', but inference is usually understood to be a cognitive process, rather than a logical relation. It's something your brain does. If you infer something, you are considering facts, ideas or assumptions and reaching one or more conclusions (i.e., you're deriving logical consequences). This process usually involves a degree of interpretation and critical reasoning.

If you're walking down the street and hear shouting, screaming and car horns honking, you might begin to worry that something bad has happened. Perhaps aliens are attacking? You can see helicopters flying overhead, and you begin to quicken your pace. Weighing up the available evidence, you could piece together a likely scenario (alien attack), which might prompt you to turn around and get out of the area as quickly as possible. Inference is the process by which you can determine and understand implications.

Of course, inferential processes can also be subject to revision. You may remember, for instance, that the local football team have just played an important match against long-standing rivals. When you listen more closely, you notice the car horns are being honked rhythmically and the shouts are, in fact, cheers. You can infer from your knowledge of your neighbours that the ruckus is a celebration of the team's win.

Inference is a type of reasoning. It requires the assessment of evidence and context, and conclusions can change depending on the evidence admitted. In general, the more information you have, the more successful your inferences are going to be.

In a nutshell
Inference is the interpretative process by which we determine and understand implications.

Why it matters
All aspects of our lives involve our ability to work out (infer), from a restricted evidence base, what might happen, what might have happened and why.

Key figures
Ruth Barcan Marcus, 1921–2012
Gottlob Frege, 1848–1925
Helen Longino, b.1944
David Wiggins, b.1933

Make the connection
rationalism, p.69
validity, p.72
know–that, p.109
conjunction, p.116

false

'True or false: the moon is made of green cheese?' True-or-false questions are questions about the state of reality. Since the moon isn't *actually* made of green cheese (or any other kind of cheese, for that matter), the statement under consideration is *false*. It isn't an accurate description of reality. We can demonstrate this through empirical investigation (try eating a moon-rock sandwich).

Falsity comes in different types. There are false statements, but there are also false promises. False promises are promises that will never be kept. Promises, which are future-oriented linguistic acts, can't always be investigated at the moment they're made. Sometimes you have to wait to find out if promises are false or not.

Unlike false statements and false promises, which require investigations into the state of the external world, *logical* falsity can be identified without recourse to observation. Something is logically false if it contradicts established truths or if its negation (its opposite) is true. The statement 'All squares have six equal sides' is logically false because it contradicts the definition of a square. A square is a polygon with four equal sides, not six, and you don't have to look at a square to know this.

When we call something false, we could be saying any number of things. We might mean that it doesn't correspond to reality, or that it's self-contradictory, or that it's inaccurate or departs from established truths. 'Falsehoods' are what we call false or misleading assertions.

In a nutshell

Falsity is the state of being incorrect or invalid.

Why it matters

It is only by distinguishing between truth and falsity that we can reliably (and safely) move through the world and rely on other people and information.

Key figures

Dorothy Edgington, b.1941
Gottlob Frege, 1848–1925
Sandra Harding, b.1935
Linda Zagzebski, b.1946

Make the connection

knowledge, p.8
objective, p.77
analysis, p.84
ontology, p.114

The moon is not made of cheese.

wrong

'Wrongness' has a broader purview than falsity. It extends beyond the realm of factual accuracy (although it can also be used to mean 'false'). We use the adjective 'wrong' to describe actions, beliefs or statements that deviate from what we consider to be morally or ethically right – i.e., justified, just or acceptable.

Crucially, wrongness – unlike falsity – is often subjective. What counts as wrong depends on your belief system – on cultural, societal or individual values. In Hinduism, for instance, it is 'wrong' to consume beef, because the cow is considered a sacred animal. The same is not true in other religions, like Christianity or Judaism.

Moreover, the same action can be considered wrong for different reasons. While some people might object to eating beef on religious grounds, others might say beef-eating is wrong because cattle farming has serious, damaging effects on the environment. Utilitarian vegetarians like Peter Singer may say it's wrong to eat meat because all lives are precious and any pleasure the beef-eater may derive from the beef-burger will be outweighed by the pain experienced by the cows.

Since wrongness is subjective, it's important to ask why this person or that person is 'in the wrong' (wherever that is). Do you agree with their view of wrongness? What exactly is their beef?

In a nutshell
To call something 'wrong' is to make a (subjective) claim about the morality of actions or beliefs.

Why it matters
Most societies have shared or overlapping understandings of wrongness. Sharing such values allows us to live (relatively) peacefully alongside each other.

Key figures
Carol J. Adams, b.1951
Alasdair MacIntyre, b.1929
Kwame Nkrumah, 1909–1972
Susan Wolf, b.1952

Make the connection
morality, p.38
ethics, p.39
realism, p.106
normal, p.134

rational

Rationality is a distinctively (if not necessarily uniquely) human cognitive achievement. It is an ability to systematically approach issues with the aim of addressing, then resolving them. Among its central features are a responsiveness to reasons and an adherence to the demands of logic.

Imagine you're being offered a new job. It's fulfilling, interesting and incredibly well paid (we can dream). However, the person offering you the job has a massive, bushy beard and you've always harboured a deep distrust of people with beards. 'Beware of long arguments and long beards,' said the essayist George Santayana. The rational response to this situation would be to take the job. You know, logically, that a beard (which can be shaved off) doesn't mean someone is untrustworthy.

More often than not, rationality is contrasted with emotion. Do you act based on facts or on 'gut instinct'? Do you follow your heart or your head? Few people nowadays think the two are so neatly separated. Indeed, many think they're deeply interlinked. Emotional engagement can be subtler and less overt, but that doesn't mean it's any less important in decision-making than rational deliberation. A deep-seated distrust of employers with beards might have less to do with Santayana's dictum than (for instance) the fact that most bearded people are men and, within misogynistic societies like our own, men are not inevitably attuned to workplace sexism.

In a nutshell
Rationality is a cognitive capacity, which involves the assessment of reasons in order to reach conclusions.

Why it matters
It's essential to robust decision-making.

Key figures
Anton Wilhelm Amo, 1703–1759
Simone de Beauvoir, 1908–1986
Michèle le Doeuff, b.1948
Emmanuel Chukwudi Eze, 1963–2007

Make the connection

I'm thinking it through.

reasonable

'Why can't you just be *reasonable?*' To be reasonable isn't simply a matter of being able to reason. We describe someone as 'reasonable' if they demonstrate a balanced and fair understanding of a situation, taking onboard opposing views and showing flexibility in interpersonal relationships. To be 'unreasonable', by contrast, is to be intractable, to resist reasoning and to doggedly pursue some aims to the exclusion of others.

Prominent in law and governmental policy, reasonableness is thought to be central to democratic engagement. In a democratic society where citizens elect governing officials, it's important to educate people to be open to other people's perspectives and arguments, and to be willing to compromise.

Critics of the concept of reasonableness, like Darren Chetty, argue that reasonableness depends on social conventions – and that these social conventions frequently sideline certain groups. In defining reasonableness, some figures are invoked more than others. In academic philosophy, for instance, there are references to 'the man on the Clapham omnibus' (a sort of everyman figure). In the United States, state legislation contains references to the 'man who mows the lawn, with his shirt sleeves rolled up'. The quintessential 'reasonable man' is, significantly, a man. Does that mean women are less reasonable? Our idea of who is and isn't reasonable can be indexed to problematic social biases.

In a nutshell
To be reasonable is, supposedly, to be balanced and open-minded, but (possibly) in ways that privilege some people over others.

Why it matters
Norms of reasonableness regulate our behaviour, interpersonally, legally and politically.

Key figures
Jody Armour
Zara Bain
Darren Chetty, b.1972
Kristie Dotson, b.1975
Alexis Shotwell, b.1974

Make the connection

infinity

I don't know about you, but infinity makes me dizzy. It's just too darn big. Whenever I think about it, my brain slips. I lose my grip. I understand what it is, in conceptual terms – an endlessness, a lack of boundaries – but I can't picture it in the same way I can picture other concepts, such as squares and triangles. Its mathematical symbol, a one-dimensional Mobiüs strip that folds in on itself (∞), isn't much help.

In mathematics, there are different types of infinity. There is, for instance, 'countable infinity'. The set of natural numbers (1, 2, 3, 4...) is countably infinite. You can keep counting them as you go, infinitely. In geometry there is also 'projective infinity'. Consider the point at which parallel lines meet. When imagined on a flat plane, parallel lines *appear* to converge on the horizon. This is 'the point at infinity', projected in the distance.

Reaching outside mathematics' disciplinary limits, discussions of the infinite are many (if not infinite). Think about infinite space. Does the universe go on and on for ever? What about qualities: can they be infinite, too? Those with a tendency towards the romantic may think that love is infinite. This isn't as hokey as it sounds. Love, both romantic and familial, is often considered to be boundless, to expand beyond limits. This is particularly the case with so-called 'unconditional' love. Other potentially infinite qualities include creativity, compassion, wisdom – and potential itself.

In a nutshell
An endlessness or boundlessness.

Why it matters
It is essential to our understanding of physics, for example, but it's an interesting question whether the concept of infinity is necessary for us to be able to go about our everyday lives.

Key figures
Anaximander, *c.*610–546 BCE
Gilles Deleuze, 1925–1995
Ibn Rushd, 'Averroes', 1126–1198
Bertrand Russell, 1872–1970

Make the connection
existence, p.70
nihilism, p.86
particle theory, p.140

eternity

'Eternity' refers to a specific type of infinity – one that relates to time. It's usually associated with the idea of time without a beginning or an end, just a temporal sloppiness (it's another slightly destabilizing thought to get your head around).

To make matters more confusing, there are different types of eternity. In a forward-looking sense, eternity can be used to describe an infinite future, though it might or might not have a starting point (e.g., the Big Bang). 'Bi-directional' eternity, by contrast, extends in both directions, into the past as well as the future.

In theological discussions, deities are sometimes described as 'eternal' (as well as infinite) and this can mean that they hang around forever (and ever), or that they exist outside time. Time – certainly linear time, which marches ever onwards in one direction – could be (like space) a feature of material reality. People who believe in immaterial objects like deities, angels and souls sometimes think that these entities are not bound by material, including temporal, limits.

Another conception of eternity involves repetition. According to the doctrine of 'eternal recurrence', all events in the universe are recurring in an infinite temporal loop. Confusingly, this type of circular eternity is apparently reliant on another, non-circular type of eternity. For us to make sense of anything repeating (including time), we have to be able to see the repetitions as part of a (chronological) series. It repeats, then repeats again, and again, and again ... *ad infinitum*.

In a nutshell
Endless time.

Why it matters
Our understanding of the universe requires us to take a position on how time works and whether or not it's infinite.

Key figures
Al-Ghazali, *c.*1058–1111
Ibn Sina, 'Avicenna', *c.*980–1037
Ibn Rushd, 'Averroes', 1126–1198
Julian of Norwich, *c.*1343–1416
Zeno, *c.*490–430 BCE

Make the connection
materialism, p.124
indeterminism, p.130
gnostic, p.138

equality

Equality refers to the state of being equal. No surprises there. Most of the time, when you hear it mentioned, it's in relation to political and legal rights. If you support gender equality, for example, you support the idea that all individuals, regardless of their gender, should have the same fundamental legal rights and access to resources.

Within sexist societies (which, let's be honest, are most societies), men and women and non-binary folk are treated differently. Within patriarchies (from the Greek, *patria-arche*, meaning 'rule of the father'), the imbalance overtly favours men. If you're a man, you are statistically more likely to get a better paid job than women and non-binary people who are similarly qualified. This is an unequal situation grounded in the perceived superiority of men.

It is only in the past few decades that some governments have attempted to address the disparities that occur in law. For example, it was after the 1975 Sex Discrimination Act was passed in the UK that women were allowed to apply for mortgages, and in 2010 that the Equality Act addressed the legal neglect of sexual harassment of women at work and in public. In 2017 it became mandatory for workplaces to report the disparities in pay between male and female employees (the so-called 'gender pay gap').

However, achieving equality does not necessarily mean treating everyone exactly the same (equally), because different individuals or groups may require different measures to address existing disparities. This leads us to the concept of equity ...

In a nutshell
The state of being equal.

Why it matters
It is an important political goal to provide the same (equal) rights and resources to everyone, regardless of their background.

Key figures
Simone de Beauvoir, 1908–1986
Anna Julia Cooper, 1858–1964
Karl Marx, 1818–1883
Paul C. Taylor, b.1967
Sojourner Truth, c.1797–1883

Make the connection
liberalism, p.47
sexism, p.48
oppression, p.52
identity politics, p.90

equity

Since people are born into different situations, equal treatment can only really be provided if resources are distributed based on individual needs. Treating people *equally* requires treating them the same (i.e., giving them the same resources). Treating people *equitably* means that resources may be allocated in a way that appears unequal. Some people, who have been disadvantaged by society, are due more than others.

Equitable treatment recognizes and attempts to rectify historical and systemic disadvantages. The aim is to provide everyone with a genuine opportunity to succeed, irrespective of their identity or their socio-economic background. Imagine a group of people trying to watch a football match over a wall. We want them all to see the game. Treating them equally, we would give them boxes of the same size to stand on, regardless of their height. This wouldn't necessarily help the shortest among them, who need larger boxes than taller people. By contrast, if we wanted to treat them equitably we would give each person a box relative in size to their height: children would have larger boxes; tall people and people wearing 1970s-style platform shoes would have smaller ones.

Equality focuses on sameness. Everyone is entitled to the same legal protections, the same access to resources, the same work opportunities. Equity emphasizes fairness and justice over sameness, and equitable treatment is treatment that acknowledges pre-existing disparities, addressing them differently in order to ensure everyone has an opportunity to succeed.

In a nutshell
Equitable treatment takes advantages and disadvantages into account in order to level a playing field.

Why it matters
Equal treatment doesn't always solve social inequality. Our policies need to be responsive to pre-existing conditions.

Key figures
Moya Bailey
Kimberlé Crenshaw, b.1959
Peggy McIntosh, b.1934
Charles W. Mills, 1951–2021

Make the connection
power, p.41
racism, p.51
prescriptive, p.74
communism, p.92

effect

One of the central preoccupations of pretty much all philosophical traditions is why stuff happens. Those with a tendency towards more technical language talk about 'causation'. Why does *this* thing cause *that* thing? Why did my comment about Alan's hairstyle make him scowl at me? And so on.

An 'effect' is what a cause causes. It is the outcome, the upshot, the consequence, the result. 'Effect' can also mean something you own (which is why we refer to 'personal effects'). Confusingly, 'effect' is a verb as well as a noun and means 'to cause' or 'to bring about': 'The manager wanted to *effect* a positive change in the workplace environment, so started wearing comedy ties.' Even more confusingly, 'to affect' can *also* mean to influence, or to change something (e.g., 'The cold weather will affect whether or not I shave my beard.')

We have developed a whole host of causal models to explain why stuff happens, why *causes* lead to *effects*. Some of these theories focus on material interactions: the pen rises into the air because I have lifted it with my hand. Others focus on the causal link between thoughts and bodily movements. How, exactly, did I cause my hand to grasp the pen and lift it? I had an intention to do so, but intentions are not obviously material objects, so how did this insubstantial cause have the desired effect?

In a nutshell
Causality refers to the relation between causes and effects. An effect is what a cause causes!

Why it matters
This is how we understand the world and our ability to interact with it.

Key figures
Democritus,
c.460–370 BCE
Jennifer Hornsby, b.1951
David Hume, 1711–1776
Helen Steward, b.1965

Make the connection

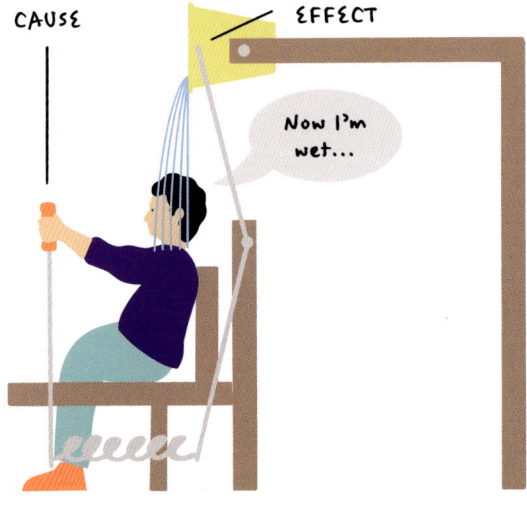

affect

As a verb, 'to affect' means 'to change' or 'to influence'. These days, we don't usually use 'affect' as a noun, but for a long time it was used to mean an emotional expression or subjective feeling. Medical doctors still sometimes talk about a patient's affect ('Their affect was cheerful while I administered the sedative.'). The word, which is etymologically and conceptually linked to the term 'affection', invokes emotions or passions.

There are clear overlaps in our different uses of 'affect'. If you're affected (moved) by a situation, a particular affect may be produced. An affect, a passion, is like an emotion – that is, a motion, a movement, a moving feeling. In this sense, an affect is an effect (though, importantly, the reverse isn't true).

Discussions of affects are prominent in Early Modern philosophical wranglings about causation. In one of the most well-known exchanges of the period, Princess Elisabeth of Bohemia questioned René Descartes about the mechanism by which the mind affected the body, producing certain affects. Questions about causation are historically linked to questions about emotion and affects.

We don't tend to speak of affects any more, at least not in our day-to-day lives, and given how confusing it is maybe that's a good thing! If you're interested in the history of emotions, however, it's helpful to be able to sort out your affects from your effects and your personal effects from your affections (to say nothing of affectations).

In a nutshell

A way of being, especially in relation to an emotional state.

Why it matters

This old-fashioned term gives us insight into the way Early Modern thinkers conceived of emotions and mental causation.

Key figures

Anton Wilhelm Amo, 1703–1759
Elisabeth of Bohemia, 1618–1680
René Descartes, 1596–1650
Baruch 'Benedict' Spinoza, 1632–1677

Make the connection

love, p.33
subjective, p.76
behaviourism, p.126

pleasure

Goodness me, life is stressful, isn't it? All evidence points to the fact that our humdrum lives are largely, if not wholly, meaningless. There's no point or purpose to them, no divine plan. On top of that, they're filled with hardship and pain, mortgages and stubbed toes. It's enough to make anyone despair.

Thoughts like these can be mitigated by 'simple pleasures', found in a variety of places: the smell of a freshly baked croissant, the sound of a child's laughter or the sight of starlings' murmurations.

'Pleasure' typically refers to sensory satisfaction, but there are forms of non-sensory, intellectual pleasure, too. Jokes, for instance. There is also that particular satisfaction you get from solving a difficult crossword clue, or the gratification you feel on remembering where you left your bus pass. Often we go in search of these pleasures. We desire them, we crave them. The satisfaction we associate with 'pleasure' is the satisfaction of a particular want or need.

One common characteristic of all these pleasures is transience. That's why we're encouraged to look for more than one simple pleasure. A single pleasure doesn't tend to last very long. Once the desire has been satisfied, that's it. The croissant has been smelled (and eaten), the pint drunk. This is one marked difference between pleasure and happiness.

In a nutshell
A typically transient enjoyable feeling.

Why it matters
Life is grim and pleasures afford us some respite.

Key figures
Teresa of Ávila, 1515–1582
Epicurus, c.341–270 BCE
Søren Kierkegaard, 1813–1855
Baruch Spinoza, 1632–1677

Make the connection
emotion, p.28
lust, p.32
liberal, p.46
aesthetic, p.120

happiness

Like pleasure, happiness is also subjective. That is, it varies from person to person, depending on their character, hopes and dreams. What makes me happy may be different from what makes you happy. Unlike pleasure, however, happiness is generally understood to be an enduring state. It's deeper, less fleeting. Your happiness, for instance, is bound up, not in a scoop of cookie-dough ice cream (nice as that is), but in your desire to become a parent, to raise a child and to see that child flourish in the world.

Happiness isn't a simple achievement – a momentary, sensory buzz. It requires reflection upon what's important – to you – and it requires you to organize your life around a set of considered values. Not only is happiness less transient, it is more holistic than pleasure. Happiness relates to you and your life as a whole. A child may take pleasure in eating cookies, while still being in a considerable amount of discomfort (having eaten three packets of cookies already). Meanwhile, someone who is happy – who is content in their job, their romantic and family life – may stub their toe, lose their wallet or fall in a hole, and remain happy.

Happiness involves meaning, meaning that is defined in relation to considered values, to how you want to live your life. By contrast, pleasure can be nothing more than a physiological response to certain external stimuli. Happiness, rather than pleasure, is close to what the Ancient Greeks called *eudaimonia*, which can be translated as 'living well'.

In a nutshell
A holistic state that tends to be the result of concerted effort and consideration of values.

Why it matters
It matters (almost by definition).

Key figures
Aristotle,
c.384–322 BCE
Confucius,
c.551–479 BCE
Christine Korsgaard,
b.1952
Martha Nussbaum,
b.1947

Make the connection

biological

Biology is the study of living things (*bios* is Greek for 'life') and biologists are primarily interested in organisms, such as enzymes, microbes, coral reefs, humans and cats. Biology encompasses a wide range of subjects, such as genetics, physiology, evolution, ecology and the study of the structure and function of cells.

The 'philosophy of biology', which is a growing subfield, examines what we mean by terms like 'species' and 'organism'. Like many such terms, the closer you look at them, the blurrier they become. What exactly makes a living being living (are viruses living, or simply self-replicating genetic tangles)? And where does an organism begin and end?

Philosophers of biology are also interested in *how* living beings exist. For a long time, distinctions have been drawn between biological entities – plants, warthogs or mushroom circles – and what are sometimes referred to as artefacts. Artefacts, which are usually made by humans (e.g., buildings, cars and Tamagotchi) are seen as, in some sense, less *real* than organisms. Organisms, which aren't dependent on humans or human society for their existence, are (putatively) more *substantial*.

Of course, developments in biotechnology may cause us to question this ruling. Biological artefacts – from bio washing powder to genetically engineered food to mice with ears on their backs – are increasingly (and perhaps disturbingly) commonplace, and increasingly blurring the boundary between human-made and biological.

In a nutshell
Concerning the study of *living* things.

Why it matters
Life (*bios*) is often used as a principle to organize the various objects we find around us, and to apportion value to them (i.e., the 'sanctity of life').

Key figures
Aristotle,
c.384–322 BCE
John Dupré, b.1952
Evelyn Fox Keller,
1936–2023
Mary Midgley,
1919–2018

Make the connection
instinct, p.34
scientific, p.96
artificial, p.105
animism, p.112

natural

There is overlap between the terms 'biological' and 'natural', and people will sometimes talk about the 'biological realm' in the same breath as the 'natural world'. There are, however, significant conceptual differences. For one thing, 'natural' entities are not always living. Mountains are natural, as are deserts and rivers and gullies. Natural phenomena include living organisms, but also geological formations and weather patterns. 'Natural' is typically used to describe processes or substances that are not influenced, created or altered by human intervention (as such, the idea of a human-made 'natural' artefact is almost a contradiction in terms).

Within a religious framework, 'natural' can take on a special meaning. If you believe in a divine Creator, then the 'natural world' – created for, and not by, humans – is a product of God's design. Since God is good (the argument goes), God's creations are good as well. This line of reasoning leads to the idea that what is natural is also good. This is why religious people, especially fundamentalists, often decry actions or attitudes as unnatural (by which they mean counter to God's wishes).

This kind of argument is a naturalistic fallacy. Just because something is natural doesn't necessarily make it good or right. It may be the case that humans naturally seek pleasure, but it requires a logical leap to stretch from this assertion to the claim that 'seeking pleasure is morally good'.

In a nutshell
The natural world is, supposedly, independent of human interference.

Why it matters
A lot of arguments – about legal, social and political matters – rely on an understanding of what is and isn't natural. For these arguments to make sense, we need to know what 'natural' means.

Key figures
Lorraine Daston, b.1951
Donna Haraway, b.1944
Ernest Nagel, 1901–1985
Susan Omaya, b.1943

Make the connection

empathy

I'm sorry to inform you that your friend's cat has just died. He was an old cat, nearing the end of his natural lifespan, but still, your friend is devastated. I daresay you can *understand* this devastation. You may even want to support your friend. But you may also be unfazed by the sudden departure of her beloved animal companion. In order to have an empathetic response to this situation, you would need to make an active effort to understand exactly how heavy your friend's loss must be. What would it be like to have a dear and supportive presence taken from you? Empathy is a complex response to someone else's situation. It requires an emotional openness and an attempt at connection. It is a cognitive process whereby a person projects themselves emotionally into another's situation.

Sometimes, declarations of empathy ring hollow. If, for instance, you're terrified about serious surgery, your friend's announcement that he 'feels your pain' because he 'once had an in-growing toenail' will probably fall wide of the mark. Empathy is characterized by a deep emotional connection, resulting from considered and careful listening and perspective-taking. Usually attributed to the nineteenth-century psychologist Theodor Lipps, the word is derived from the German *einfülung*, meaning 'feeling into'. For some thinkers, like Edith Stein and Simone Weil, empathy is a kind of 'affective resonance' – a genuine instance of a shared emotion and an intrinsic part of our ethical engagement with our fellow humans.

In a nutshell
An emotional response in which one person understands another person's pain almost as if it were their own.

Why it matters
It allows us to offer support to family and friends and to feel closer to them.

Key figures
N. Katherine Hayles, b.1943
Rae Langton, b.1961
Sojourner Truth, *c.*1797–1883
Simone Weil, 1909–1943

Make the connection

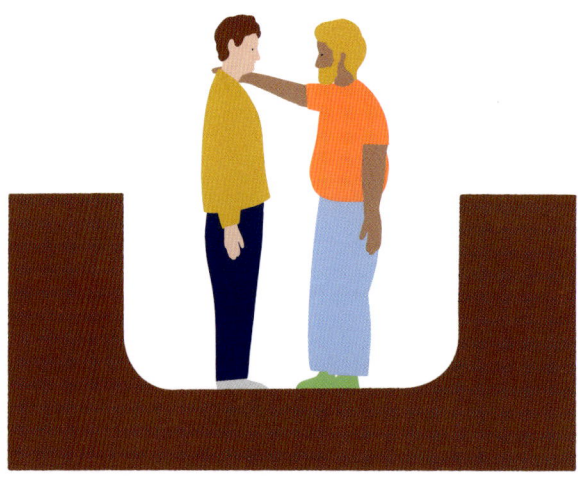

sympathy

One of the reasons sympathy and empathy are used interchangeably is that 'sympathy', an older word, was once much closer in meaning to our modern understanding of empathy. Originating in the Greek *sympatheia* (meaning 'fellow feeling' or 'shared feeling'), the term has historically been used to describe how individuals *enter into* the feelings of others. For this reason, many pre-nineteenth-century Anglophone texts use sympathy and make no mention of empathy.

Nowadays, however, 'sympathy' refers to a less obviously involved emotional response than empathy. When you're being sympathetic, you need not actually share in a feeling. Rather, a sympathetic individual is simply acknowledging and expressing concern for someone else's feelings or difficulties. Such responses often manifest as expressions of comfort ('There, there…') and condolences ('I'm very sorry for your loss'). Unlike empathy, this use of sympathy involves a compassionate acknowledgement of another person's emotions without any need for those emotions to be shared.

These two terms are now generally understood to have distinct meanings, but variations in usage can still be found in philosophical and psychological literature. The distinction is not always rigidly maintained (especially in contemporary commentary on eighteenth- and nineteenth-century texts). These terms, like all of the words in this book, are a product of ongoing linguistic evolution. Which is to say: use them carefully.

In a nutshell
The supportive acknowledgement of someone else's hardship.

Why it matters
It provides a foundation for interpersonal support and solidarity.

Key figures
Philippa Foot, 1920–2010
Baruch Spinoza, 1632–1677
Simone Weil, 1909–1943
Sylvia Wynter, b.1928

Make the connection

emotion

A lot of us get angry when we watch the news. When we hear about the corrupt politicians and exploitative businesses, we feel our blood boiling. Our heart rates increase, fists clench, and our thoughts start skipping from one horrible thing to another. Anger – like sadness, fear, disgust and love – is an emotion, a complex psychological and physiological response to a specific stimulus or situation.

Within certain philosophical traditions, emotional engagement is understood to be in conflict with rational deliberation. In many of the canonical works of European philosophy, emotions are thought to cloud rational judgement (and as such, to be obstructive to good philosophizing). The ideal philosopher is (it's claimed) someone who can put their emotions to one side and puzzle through a problem using pure logic. Unfortunately, because of longstanding sexist associations between women and emotions, which also paint rationality as a distinctively masculine achievement, this attitude has contributed to the mistaken and pernicious belief that women are irrational (and make for poor philosophers). Hence Immanuel Kant's unpleasant remark that 'a woman who has her head full of Greek may as well have a beard into the bargain.'

While this coarse split between emotion and reason persists, it is increasingly challenged in the philosophical mainstream. Not only are gendered associations called into question, but feminist thinkers like Nel Noddings examine the degree to which emotions can be central to rational deliberation.

In a nutshell
Emotions are those feelings, like anger, happiness and sadness, which colour our engagement with each other and the world.

Why it matters
Comprehensible or not, emotions enrich our lives, bringing happiness and joy (as well as sadness and fear).

Key figures
Patricia Hill Collins, b.1948
Nel Noddings, 1929–2022
Baruch Spinoza, 1632–1677

Make the connection
rational, p.14
affect, p.21
empathy, p.26
love, p.33

mood

Emotions are responses to specific stimuli or situations. Moods, however, are understood to be more general, more enduring and less targeted. When I'm grumpy, for instance, I'm rarely grumpy about any one thing. There's no specific cause, I just 'woke up on the wrong side of the bed'. I'm grumpy and everything I encounter is the subject of my grumpiness: the birds are chirping too cheerily, the coffee pot is bubbling too loudly, there's too much (or possibly too little) peanut butter on my toast. I'm just *grumpy*, okay?

A mood is a general feeling, which expands and attaches to the objects and people around you. You can be dour, irritable or anxious and these can be 'frames of mind' rather than direct responses to specific stimuli. A philosopher of mind might say that moods, in contrast to emotions, do not have 'intentional objects'. Moods have vaguer boundaries than emotions. Flashes of anger or pangs of love are relatively easy to identify (they are discrete, boundaried), but anxiety and other such moods *creep*. They can sneak up on you unaware, and they can affect your emotional interactions. If you're in an irritable mood, you may be quicker to anger. If you're in an anxious frame of mind, you may cry more quickly. Emotions are focused, whereas moods can be harder to identify and often arise in obscure ways.

In a nutshell
A more general and less targeted feeling, such as a 'malaise' (ill-at-easeness).

Why it matters
These background feelings affect the way we interact with the world and each other.

Key figures
Sara Ahmed, b.1969
Peter Goldie, 1946–2011
Richard Wollheim, 1923–2003

Make the connection
affect, p.21
ideology, p.66
consciousness, p.88
phenomenology, p.118
intentionality, p.129

sarcasm

Within the sphere of aesthetics, the area of academic philosophy that focuses on issues of art, beauty and culture, there is the rather surprising subfield known as the 'philosophy of humour'. People working in this area examine jokes (and comedy in general) in order to develop theories in answer to questions such as: Why is humour a central part of our social lives? Why do we find things funny? Are some jokes morally wrong? Are they morally wrong even if they're hilarious? What if they're *really* hilarious?

Despite being 'the lowest form of wit', sarcasm is still open to philosophical analysis. It's a speech act that involves saying something with the intention of conveying the opposite meaning. This is typically achieved with the use of a mocking or scornful tone. Words are drawn out and exaggerated to make it apparent that the speaker is saying something contrary to what they think: 'That's *so* fascinating, *do* tell me more.'

Sarcasm is usually deployed to express negative emotions, such as contempt or frustration. The word comes from the Greek verb *sarkazein*, which, translated literally, means 'to tear flesh'. It involves metaphorical cutting, wounding and biting (which is why we talk of 'biting remarks'). Sarcastic comments, even ones made in jest, are a form of attack. They can be playful (made between friends) or vindictive. They can even be expressions of resistance (and, helpfully, since sarcasm is primarily tonal, it's easy to pretend you haven't been sarcastic when you have).

In a nutshell
A form of humour used to change the literal meaning of a statement.

Why it matters
Since sarcasm can dramatically change the meaning of a sentence without changing the words, we need to be able to recognize it in order to avoid confusion. Also, it's funny.

Key figures
Roxane Gay, b.1974
Søren Kierkegaard, 1813–1855
Toni Morrison, 1931–2019
Catharine Trotter Cockburn, 1679–1749

Make the connection
contradiction, p.64
ideology, p.66
nihilism, p.86
aesthetic, p.120

irony

Sarcasm is a form of verbal irony, but there are other types of irony too. Situations can be ironic (but not sarcastic). Imagine, for instance, an animal-rights activist being killed by one of the lions they've spent their life trying to save. There is dramatic irony as well, and cosmic irony, Socratic irony and even something called litotes, which is a rhetorical device whereby an affirmative is expressed by negating its opposite, using understatement for emphasis, e.g. 'Well, I'm not *un*-happy.'

Irony involves incongruity, an out-of-placeness or inappropriateness. As a figure of speech, irony emphasizes a contrast between the literal meaning of words and their intended meaning. If I look at the pouring rain and say, 'Oh what a beautiful day', there is a pointed disconnect between reality and my assessment of it. A situation is described as ironic if the outcome it describes is relatively unexpected. If the fire station burns down while the firefighters are saving a cat stuck in a tree, there is a noticeable discrepancy between the anticipated outcome of the firefighters' work and the real outcome.

For some philosophers of humour, incongruity is a central source of comedy. The surprise, the cognitive dissonance that results when you're expecting one thing and experience another, can be pleasurable or funny or both. Some people think irony's ability to subvert expectations can be politically useful because it draws attention to assumptions. In so doing it can encourage a re-evaluation of those preconceived notions.

In a nutshell
A linguistic mode that involves pointed incongruity or inappropriateness, often to humorous effect.

Why it matters
It's one of the most pleasurable and subtlest forms of human interaction.

Key figures
Sara Ahmed, b.1969
Søren Kierkegaard, 1813–1855
Arthur Schopenhauer, 1788–1860
Paul C. Taylor, b.1967

Make the connection
pleasure, p.22
oppression, p.52
hegemony, p.67

lust

Loosen your collar and suspend your propriety, lust is one of the steamiest areas of philosophical inquiry. It's a powerful human emotion – a visceral and overwhelming urge typically associated with sexual desire. It's a common feeling, a normal part of human experience – sometimes fleeting, sometimes felt in the initial stages of romantic relationships – but for all its ubiquity it's frequently viewed in a negative light. According to some strands of Christian theology, for instance, lust is one of the seven deadly sins (alongside heavy hitters like wrath and avarice).

There are different reasons lust is thought to be problematic and why it's prohibited by many religions. In the Abrahamic faiths – Judaism, Christianity and Islam – sex and sexual desire are very carefully policed. Lust is thought to lead people to contravene religious and social contracts (e.g., breaking marriage vows or, shock horror, masturbating!) Part of the reason lust is seen to be dangerous is that it is overwhelming. It supposedly undermines an individual's self-control. It clouds judgement and disturbs the ability to reason (or so the argument goes).

Lust is described as an urge to *have* something, to *possess* it. This may seem a little troubling if the object of the lust is a person. Generally speaking, we don't think people should be possessions. So lust may be considered problematic if it leads you to think of someone (maybe even a stranger) as something other than a person – as simply an object, a collection of physical attributes that you find attractive.

In a nutshell
A desire (often sexual) to have or possess something or someone.

Why it matters
Most people, at some point in their lives, experience some form of lust.

Key figures
Carol J. Adams, b.1951
Teresa of Ávila, 1515–1582
Rae Langton, b.1961
Uma Narayan, b.1958
Virginia Woolf, 1882–1941

Make the connection

love

Imagine listening to a friend constantly talking about their new partner. They're always singing his praises, waxing lyrical about his chiselled jaw, his windswept hair, the swirling butterflies they feel in their stomach when they see him. Imagine your friend only ever mentioning his physical attributes (those muscles, those abs). You may wonder if they're in love, or simply in lust.

Unlike lust, love is understood to be a profound and multifaceted emotion, characterized by care and connection, emotional intimacy and a genuine concern for the wellbeing of someone else. Romantic love is just one type of love, alongside familial love, self-love and more general feelings, like the love of humanity. You can love your friends as well, which is sometimes called Platonic love.

There is also religious love. The medieval Christian mystic Julian of Norwich is best known for her *Revelations of Divine Love*, in which she explores the different elements of God's love for humans, and her own love of God and Christ. She frequently uses maternal imagery: God's love is motherly – unconditional, nurturing and compassionate (contrast this with the almost lustful writings of Teresa of Ávila).

Love and lust are typically put in opposition but, as ever, reality is not so neatly divided. Our emotions, urges and desires can, theoretically, be categorized, but the fluidity of experience is rarely so easily understood.

In a nutshell
A complex, multifaceted emotion, characterized by care and connection.

Why it matters
Love connects us to others and underpins a large number of social institutions (such as marriage and the family).

Key figures
Gloria Anzaldúa, 1942–2004
Clare Chambers, b.1976
bell hooks, 1952–2021
Plato, *c.*428–423 BCE

Make the connection
happiness, p.23
emotion, p.28
mood, p.29
rite, p.55

instinct

You're walking home and a mysterious figure runs at you out of a doorway. You instinctively draw back. You may even run away or throw a punch. Fortunately, it turns out to be a friend who saw you through the window and wanted to say hello.

When we describe actions as instinctive, we're suggesting that they are unthinking. It's your body taking over, reacting, perhaps, with a fixed pattern of 'fight or flight' behaviour. Instincts are usually understood to be innate behaviours that have developed as a response to adaptive pressures. There are plenty of them in the biological world. Many bird species exhibit the instinct to migrate and nest, while carnivores possess a strong hunting instinct (a 'killer' instinct) and a tendency to bare their teeth or claws when in danger.

If we're being biologically precise, an instinct is a type of physiological behaviour, but we're not always biologically precise, and 'instinct' means other things too. Colloquially, an instinctive reaction is one performed without consideration: it's a knee-jerk response (a knee-jerk, by the way, is a type of instinctive reaction known as a reflex). In this sense, 'instinct' can refer to any action that occurs without conscious thought. Say you've gone through rigorous military training before your friend jumps out at you. Your instinct may be to draw a weapon or otherwise attack the perceived threat. This is learned behaviour, the result of extended and repeated practice. Instinct can mean learned reflexes, 'muscle memory', as well as innate biological imperative.

In a nutshell
Either a learned or innate 'knee-jerk' response.

Why it matters
It's important to know which forces govern our actions. It can be emotions, or rational deliberation or instinct (and other things besides).

Key figures
René Descartes, 1596–1650
Mary Midgley, 1919–2018
Iris Murdoch, 1919–1999
Beverly Daniel Tatum, b.1954

Make the connection
biological, p.24
behaviourism, p.126
intention, p.128
agency, p.147

intuition

As every aspiring private detective knows, it's important to listen to your gut. But gut instinct isn't an instinct in either of the senses already described. It isn't just physiological. It involves a degree of decision-making and an interpretation of the social world. Strictly speaking, gut instinct is actually an intuition.

An intuition is a perceived insight that isn't necessarily based on conscious thought or explicit reasoning. It's a hunch. A suspicion. An inclination. It's not a physical reflex or a biological reaction. It's a cognitive response.

An intuition can function as a useful mental shorthand for more complicated processes. Consider a medic in the middle of a difficult and time-sensitive surgical procedure. She has to make a split-second decision and doesn't have time to weigh up the various pros and cons. If the doctor is sufficiently well trained and practised, you might think her intuitions are at least *semi*-reliable guides to these emergency actions.

Unfortunately, unlike instincts, intuitions can be wrong. Your intuitive understanding of a situation may be based on mistaken information (for example, the doctor may not know the patient is a haemophiliac). Even when, like 'female intuition', they're framed as biological instincts, intuitions are more often than not the result of socialization (i.e., how we're trained to be in society). It's clear from the sociological data that intuitions vary across cultures. And if our intuitions vary across culture and someone's culture is politically regressive, then their intuitions may be less progressive than in other parts of the world.

In a nutshell
A perceived insight, which doesn't require explicit conscious reasoning.

Why it matters
We use intuitions to navigate the world, but sometimes they can prejudice against certain people and encourage us to favour others.

Key figures
Daniel Dennett, 1942–2024
Michel Foucault, 1926–1984
Sally Haslanger, b.1955
Shirley Anne Tate, b.1956

Make the connection

I've got a hunch about this.

sex

Polite society tends to frown on people who talk openly about sex, which is probably quite a good reason to do so. 'Sex' can refer to the act of sexual intercourse but when contrasted with gender, the word refers to a certain set of anatomical attributes that we typically categorize as male or female. Medical science usually bases this classification on the appearance of external genitalia. If you have a penis, you're a male; if you have a vagina, you're a female. Historically, we have used this binary to organize humans into men and women and to classify other animals, too (though the biological world has any number of examples that challenge this simple distinction, from seahorses to flatworms and starfish).

The binary model of sex is central to much mainstream medical science, but biologists are increasingly arguing that it's an oversimplification. Some individuals are born 'intersex', which means that their biological attributes – such as genitalia or chromosomal patterns – do not fit standard definitions of male or female. Interestingly, a number of biological attributes appear internally. Someone with a vagina may also have internal testes; someone with a penis may also have internal ovarian tissue. Consequently, it's not immediately obvious whether or not someone is intersex. Indeed, they might not even know themselves. All of this is to say that sex is far from a strict binary. It's a continuum along which humans can fall.

In a nutshell
Sex is (among other things) a biological classification based on physical attributes.

Why it matters
The binary model of sex organizes our societies, often determining the kind of work you can pursue and your life chances.

Key figures
Sara Ahmed, b.1969
Michel Foucault, 1926–1984
Judith Jack Halberstam, b.1961
bell hooks, 1952–2021

Make the connection
biological, p.24
sexism, p.48
medical ontology, p.115

gender

In contrast to sex, gender encompasses social, cultural and psychological attributes. Being a man or a woman isn't about biology, but about the performance of certain roles, identities and behaviours. Being masculine or feminine isn't to do with your genitals, it's to do with the way you dress, how you act, how you engage with the world.

Historically, many societies have tended to see a strict connection between biological sex and gender. People with penises are men, while people with vaginas are women. However, recognizing that gender is a performance encourages us to question this connection. You might identify with the gender assigned to you at birth by the doctor – that would make you 'cisgender' – but you might not. Your gender identity can differ from your perceived biological sex. Transgender people resist the assessment made at their birth, which was based on their observable genitals.

Non-binary people resist the assumption that gender (like biological sex) is a strict binary. You don't have to be either a man or a woman. You might not identify particularly strongly with either masculine or feminine traits or you might identify with both – or with some at some points, and others at other points. Sex is a biological concept focused on physiological attributes, whereas gender encompasses the social, cultural and psychological dimensions of being, for instance, a woman. Importantly, the strict binaries of both gender and sex can be questioned. The world has fewer clear-cut distinctions than many would have us believe.

In a nutshell
A performance of particular types of identity, such as masculine or feminine.

Why it matters
Separating gender from sex allows us to better understand and explore our identities.

Key figures
Simone de Beauvoir, 1908–1986
Talia Mae Bettcher
Judith Butler, b.1956
Sophie-Grace Chappell, b.1964

Make the connection
natural, p.25
intersectionality, p.91
normal, p.134

morality

Morality is a code of conduct – a set of principles and values. Morality is everywhere, which doesn't mean that everyone is always 'moral', a term often used to mean 'good', since we clearly aren't. It means we live in societies organized by codes of conduct, whether we subscribe to them or not.

Sometimes the term morality refers to the set of principles and values established by a specific group. At the heart of a Christian morality there is a particular idea of an all-loving and all-knowing God. But 'morality' can also be seen in a more far-reaching way to include principles for all rational beings to follow. A Christian, a Muslim and an atheist may have different moral systems, but all might agree that murder is wrong. This means that 'moral judgements' sometimes seem to apply to everyone.

The moral systems we construct might acknowledge that certain judgements are universal, but there might also be mitigating circumstances. While everyone thinks murder is wrong (perhaps by definition), some *may* believe murder is allowed in specific circumstances. Murder is common on the battlefield, so is typically thought to be acceptable in this context.

In a nutshell
The difference between what is 'right' and what is 'wrong'.

Why it matters
Morality is everywhere. Whether we adhere to them or not, there are codes of conduct by which we, and the societies we live in, are organized.

Key figures
Hannah Arendt, 1906–1975
Augustine, c.354–430 CE
Iris Murdoch, 1919–1999

Make the connection
wrong, p.13
rationality, p.14
being good, p.45
ideology, p.66

ethics

Often, ethics is understood to be the art of 'living well'. Your ethics are about your attitude to the world, your character and your personal development. Your ethical stance refers to the virtues you exemplify, the values you hold most dear and how you act on them in the world. The reach of ethics is broader than morality, which focuses on principles and judgements.

Which ethics do you live by? You may be kind, gentle, decisive, courageous, contemplative, determined or flexible. None of these is necessarily better or worse than the others, they're not 'right' or 'wrong', they're just different ways of approaching the situations you find yourself in. You might, for instance, have a strong work ethic, which emphasizes hard work and diligence in your day-to-day existence. Or you may have a more relaxed ethos and attitude to life, putting an emphasis on keeping things 'chill'.

Morality refers to an abstract system of principles and laws. Ethics is the way we embody that abstract system, how it figures in our attitudes to others, and how we bring it to life.

In a nutshell
The art of 'living well'.

Why it matters
Ethics is the manner in which we choose to live and treat people. Your ethics are formed by your character, your personal development and your attitude to the world.

Key figures
Martin Luther King, 1929–1968
Christine Korsgaard, b.1952
Martha Nussbaum, b.1947

Make the connection
happiness, p.23
natural, p.25
relativism, p.107

privilege

As a white, able-bodied man in British society, I have certain unearned advantages – privileges – that can make my life easier than other people's. I am statistically less likely than Black men to be stopped and searched by the police; I am more likely to be promoted at work than women in the same role; and compared to a wheelchair-user I have much greater access to public services. I haven't earned these privileges. I have them simply by virtue of having a certain identity in a certain type of society.

All too often, privileges like these go unnoticed and unexamined. Instead, people may describe their position in society as 'natural', or a result of their innate brilliance. The anti-racist activist and research scientist Peggy McIntosh describes 'white privilege' as an invisible knapsack that white people are carry around with them. The knapsack contains the daily effects of white privilege. For example: 'I can turn on the television and see people of my race widely represented.' On the whole, white people brought up in white families and majority-white education systems aren't encouraged to unpack the invisible knapsack they carry around. Intentionally or not, we can avoid looking at our privileges because to do so involves recognizing that the world is a much more complicated, and a much harder, place for other people. It's much easier to believe that we're great than to think our successes are down to identity characteristics.

In a nutshell
An unearned social advantage.

Why it matters
Societies that automatically grant privileges to some and not others are unequal.

Key figures
bell hooks, 1952–2021
Zeus Leonardo
Audre Lorde, 1934–1992
Charles W. Mills, 1951–2021

Make the connection

power

To be privileged is to have a kind of power. Privileges can open doors and break glass ceilings. The focus on privileges, however, can direct attention onto individuals rather than towards the systems and structures from which the power actually stems.

In mainstream public discourse, a lot of anti-racist work involves 'checking one's privileges' (or examining 'unconscious bias'). White people are encouraged to consider all the ways they are given advantages simply by virtue of being white. This kind of consciousness raising is clearly important, but the implication is that anti-Black racism can be addressed by individuals.

American educator Zeus Leonardo argues that the concept of white privilege is insufficient for effective anti-racist action. Not only does it imply that white people are simply ignorant of (and therefore not responsible for) their advantages, it draws attention from the structures that teach white people to ignore the systems invested in white empowerment. White people don't simply have 'unconscious biases'; we are actively invested in ignoring our whiteness.

Traditionally 'white power', like 'white supremacy', has been taken to refer to extremist and explicitly anti-Black groups and movements. Like author and theorist bell hooks, Leonardo suggests there are more insidious forms of white empowerment, embedded in our everyday lives and all the more powerful for being unseen.

In a nutshell
A social force.

Why it matters
Understanding the difference between power and privilege is central to combatting systemic oppressions.

Key figures
Kimberlé Crenshaw, b.1959
Kristie Dotson, b.1975
Zeus Leonardo
Kwame Nkrumah, 1909–1972

Make the connection
racism, p.51
oppression, p.52
identity politics, p.90
consciousness raising, p.137

race

'Race' is one of the many ways we categorize people. We might say of someone, 'She's Black' or 'He's white', and by doing so we're drawing attention to a perceived difference based on physical characteristics such as skin colour, facial features, hair texture and other anatomical features. For a long time, it has been assumed that these categories (such as white, Black and Asian) correspond to real, biological categories (subspecies). This assumption, sometimes referred to as 'race science' or 'scientific racism', has been the foundation for racist policies and laws that see some groups as naturally (biologically) inferior or superior to others.

Modern science, however, recognizes that these categories do not reflect biological reality. There is no Black gene or white gene. Indeed, the genetic diversity *within* racial groups can be as significant as the diversity *between* them. Certainly our traits can be explained biologically, but the lack of melanin in my skin, which makes me appear 'white' (pinky yellow-ish), is just one feature of my complex, tangled genetic inheritance.

Rather than thinking that race is a biological term, many now see it as a social construction. Racial difference is created (constructed) and defined by societies. It's imposed externally on individuals, often – maybe always – in a way that preserves certain power structures. If you are designated as 'white' within a white supremacist society, you will benefit from more powers and privileges than if you are designated as a person 'of colour'.

In a nutshell
A social construct once believed to have a biological basis.

Why it matters
Race is one of the many ways in which people attempt to justify systems of oppression.

Key figures
Anna Julia Cooper, 1858–1964
W. E. B. Du Bois, 1868–1963
Frantz Fanon, 1925–1961
Paul C. Taylor, b.1967

Make the connection
racism, p.51
identity politics, p.90
double consciousness, p.136

ethnicity

Like race, ethnicity is socially constructed, and it encapsulates an even greater number of traits, both physical and non-physical. Ethnicity refers to shared cultural characteristics, including language, ancestry, customs and a sense of common history. It can, but doesn't always, include reference to how people look.

For example, I'm usually racialized as 'white', which is to say that British society currently sees me as white. However, at other times I might be positioned as ethnically Jewish. As an Ashkenazi Jew, I have ancestors from particular regions of Eastern Europe, where they lived in specific communities with shared customs and some shared genetic traits (although, importantly, I share these genetic traits with other Eastern Europeans who wouldn't be categorized as Jewish). To make matters more complicated, people can be considered Jewish by virtue of converting to the religion Judaism. You needn't be ethnically Jewish in order to be considered 'Jewish', because the term encompasses a religious orientation. And you don't need to be a religious Jew to be ethnically Jewish. You can be born into a Jewish family with a particular cultural inheritance without also practising the religion.

Given how confusing this all is, it's unsurprising that questions about race and ethnicity are often controversial. Definitions of race and ethnicity like the ones above are often hotly contested, because they're social constructions and societies (tragically, and inevitably) don't always construct things in clear or well-articulated ways.

In a nutshell
Another social construction used to group people. It can refer to a collection of physical and non-physical traits.

Why it matters
Like race, ethnicity is one of the many ways that people are grouped together, sometimes to their political advantage and sometimes their disadvantage.

Key figures
Emmanuel Levinas, 1906–1995
Edward Said, 1935–2003
Gayatri Spivak, b.1942
Shirley Anne Tate, b.1956

Make the connection
privilege, p.40
oppression, p.52
essential, p.62
'philosophy', p.154

doing good

It's good to do good things, right? This seems self-evidently true, and many of our moral and ethical theories reflect this. Most of us assume that morality involves, maybe even fundamentally, the ability to 'do good' in the world.

In some sense, 'doing good' is a matter of causing good things to happen. Good is 'done' if you manage to help people, increase happiness, relieve suffering or create the conditions for peace and harmony. In this sense, doing good is focused on the *consequences* of one's actions.

If you're interested in good deeds, then you'll tend to evaluate the morality of an action based on outcomes. If you're calculating 'the right thing to do', you'll look at an action's effects in the world. If performing mouth-to-mouth resuscitation means you save a life, it's a good thing to do. If leaving your car running while it's parked contributes to global warming, then it's a bad thing to do. Utilitarians, who focus on the 'utility' of their actions for the general good, emphasize the importance of good outcomes.

This kind of moral assessment can end up as a sort of cost-benefit analysis. Imagine, for instance, that a local council is asked to approve a large-scale industrial project. This so-called 'consequentialist' reasoning involves looking at the consequences of such a project: it may create more jobs, but it will also pollute the local ecosystem. If you're interested in 'doing' good (the *greatest* good), then you need to work out and compare the potential consequences.

In a nutshell
Some moral systems – such as consequentialism – focus on *doing* the right thing, highlighting the result of an action rather than the action itself.

Why it matters
Assessing the value of our actions' consequences is one of the main ways we decide what to do.

Key figures
G. E. M. Anscombe, 1919–2001
Jeremy Bentham, 1748–1832
Anita Silvers, 1940–2019
Peter Singer, b.1946

Make the connection
effect, p.20
morality, p.38
rote, p.54

being good

Given that we think doing good is good, it's strange that we use 'do-gooder' as an insult. It suggests that there's something a little suspicious about *doing* good – and on reflection, maybe there is. The phrase 'do-gooder' carries a hint of smug self-righteousness; it highlights the degree to which doing good can be a performance. We call people do-gooders if they're making a show of their good deeds, and there are plenty of non-moral and actively immoral reasons to *act* as if you're a moral person. The performance of good deeds can actually be used to disguise other, less moral activities.

In contrast to consequentialist moral theories, 'virtue ethics' emphasizes the development of a virtuous character. The primary aim is not to do good things, but to *be* good – to think about the values and virtues you want to embody (charity, courage, generosity and so forth) and to embody them. Virtue ethics recognizes that sometimes you can do good things and be immoral, and you can be a moral person and cause bad things to happen.

The distinction between the two approaches, between doing good and being good, is clear in our political landscape. Politicians try very hard to appear to do good things and sometimes they succeed. Their motivations are obscure, however. 'Principled' politicians act primarily according to their values rather than popular opinion, which is admirable but lessens the chance of being re-elected and doing greater good in the long-term.

In a nutshell
Virtue ethics focuses on the goodness of an act rather than the goodness of its consequences.

Why it matters
What's good and bad is more than a cost–benefit analysis of consequences. In significant ways, it's the thought that counts.

Key figures
Aristotle, *c.*384–322 BCE
Confucius, *c.*551–479 BCE
Christine Korsgaard, b.1952
Martha Nussbaum, b.1947

Make the connection
happiness, p.23
ethics, p.39
prescriptive, p.74
relativism, p.107

liberal

Vegan custard is surprisingly good these days. Whenever I make an apple crumble (which is often), I apply the vegan custard *liberally*. My friends might say I apply it too liberally, since there's usually more custard than crumble. 'Liberal', in this everyday sense, means 'generously', or without particular inhibitions. I'm very permissive when it comes to the application of custard.

The word 'liberal' can mean something similar when we're talking about our political views. To say that someone has 'a liberal approach' to parenting means that they aren't overly strict or restrictive in bringing up a child. Being a liberal parent implies being flexible when enforcing rules and encouraging independence. Less liberal (or actively illiberal) parents may worry this kind of flexibility – a *laissez faire* attitude to childcare – may be too unstructured. Consequently, they may be more disciplinarian, relying on rule-following and punishment (discipline) to raise the kids.

'Liberal' is also used as a synonym for 'progressive', which may be because liberal people can be open-minded and flexible (liberal) regarding new ideas, where illiberal folk are more conservative. This use of liberal is common in politics. Having a liberal attitude toward different cultural practices means that you're open to them. Liberal can mean generous, permissive, unrestricted, flexible, progressive, open-minded and tolerant. We use it, liberally, in different contexts.

In a nutshell
Can mean generous or permissive.

Why it matters
It can be important to be open-minded (liberal) when interacting with people who don't share the same views as you.

Key figures
Hannah Arendt, 1906–1975
José Medina
Desmond Tutu, 1931–2021

Make the connection
prejudice, p.50
socialism, p.93
consciousness raising, p.137

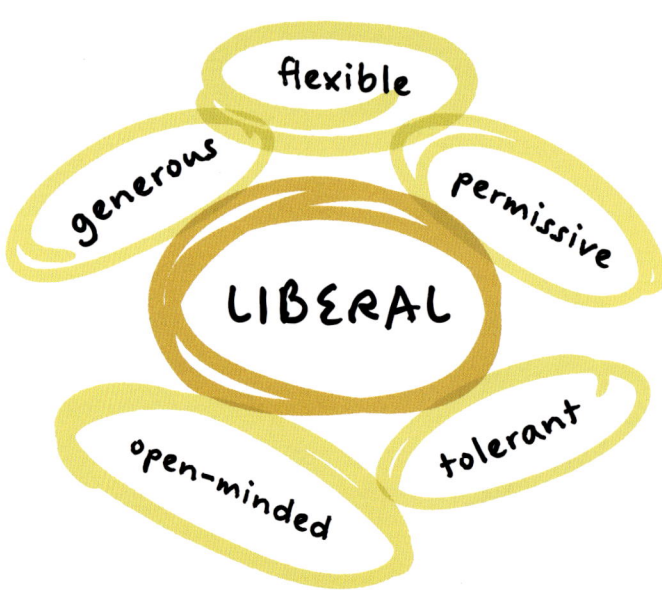

liberalism

Unfortunately (and confusingly), the term 'liberal' is used in a different, more specific sense in the political sphere. Liberalism, the doctrine to which political liberals adhere, is a particular political philosophy that emphasizes the importance of individual rights, freedom, equality and the rule of law. Liberalism holds that citizens should be free (at liberty) to do what they want to do, as much as is practically possible. This means, for example, that liberals advocate for limited government intervention. They think state bodies should be involved only minimally in our private lives. Liberals also prioritize the protection of individual rights, such as free speech, and the separation of the church and the state (to protect religious freedom and prevent the imposition of religions on citizens).

Political liberals also support the 'rule of law'. They think a just and orderly society depends on laws, and that the laws should be applied equally to everyone. Because they tend to want to limit government intervention, most of the laws they favour are organized around the 'Harm Principle', found in its canonical form in the nineteenth-century texts of John Stuart Mill and Harriet Taylor, which holds that power can only be exercised over citizens if doing so prevents harm to others.

Liberalism is not necessarily 'liberal' in the sense of being progressive. The political liberal aims to leave citizens to their own devices, which can include (for example) strict parenting, as well as illiberal views about the application of custard to crumble.

In a nutshell
The view that people should be at liberty to do as they please as long as it doesn't cause harm to themselves or others.

Why it matters
It is possibly the dominant political ideology in the world.

Key figures
Kwame Anthony Appiah, b.1954
Thomas Hobbes, 1588–1679
Charles W. Mills, 1951–2021
Jean-Jacques Rousseau, 1712–1778

Make the connection
communism, p.92
neo-liberalism, p.99
autocracy, p.102

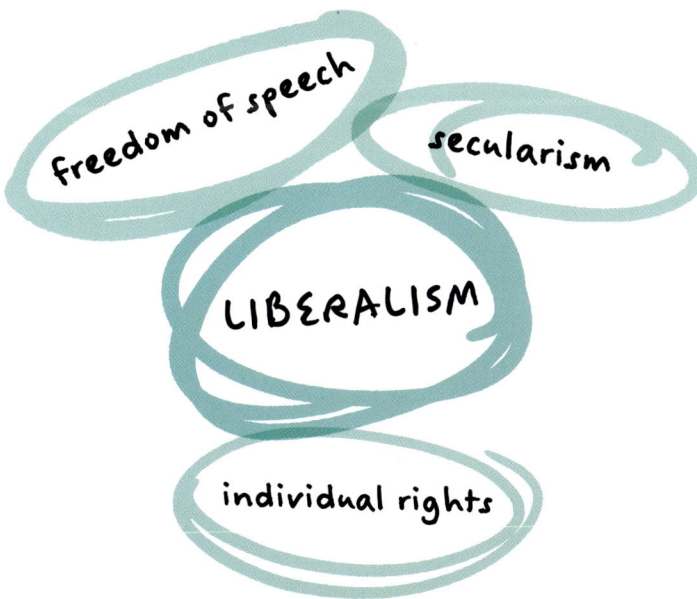

sexism

Sexism refers to discrimination or prejudice based on sex. Technically, it can be directed towards anyone. In reality, however, it is primarily directed towards women. It is a collection of beliefs (e.g., that men are more rational than women) and practices (e.g., inequalities in pay) that contribute to the subordination of one group to another.

Sexism can manifest at the individual and institutional level. An example of interpersonal sexism might be 'mansplaining', where a man explains something to a woman in the mistaken belief that, because he is a man, he understands the subject better than she does. Institutional sexism formalizes these beliefs into policy. 'Men only' clubs are sexist because they discriminate against women *as* women.

Importantly, while much sexism is overtly hostile, it can also be apparently benevolent and performed with good intentions. A man opening a door for a woman and announcing 'Ladies first' appears well intentioned, but the action invokes the belief that women are fragile, weak and in need of men.

Sexist societies, which are most, if not all, societies, enforce a hierarchy on the grounds of sex and gender. Men are placed at the top and everyone else is below them. Such societies are called patriarchies, from the Greek *pater*, meaning 'father', and *archein*, meaning 'to govern'.

In a nutshell
Discrimination based on sex.

Why it matters
It describes the way women are oppressed as women. As such, it is an important conceptual tool for understanding and protecting women's rights.

Key figures
Sara Ahmed, b.1969
Simone de Beauvoir, 1908–1986
Kate Manne, b.1983
Sojourner Truth, c.1797–1883

Make the connection
rational, p.14
privilege, p.40
domination, p.53

misogyny

The word 'misogyny' is also Greek in origin and comes from the words *misos*, meaning 'hatred', and *gyne*, meaning 'woman' ('misandry' is the hatred of men, *andros*). While sexism involves discriminatory practices and beliefs, misogyny is characterized by a deep-seated hatred and contempt for women. Insults that liken women to animals, for instance, are demeaning and suggest disgust.

Sexism and misogyny are not 'natural' attitudes. They're part of a political ideology – patriarchy. According to the philosopher Kate Manne, the function of misogyny is to enforce sexist attitudes by punishing and controlling women who defy them. Consider the sexist belief that women are supposed to be demure and deferential to men's needs. Women who reject this belief, who pursue sexual liberation, are defying traditional gender roles. Within a patriarchy, their actions are punished through practices such as 'slut-shaming'. Misogyny is a way of keeping women 'in their place'.

Sexism and misogyny are directed towards women (sexism towards intersex people, also, and sometimes men), but patriarchal societies negatively impact everyone. When traditional gender roles are policed, when people are forced to meet certain social expectations, they are denied choice. This is true even when they also benefit from certain privileges. Within a patriarchy, men must conform to types just as much as women. The risks are fewer, but they still stand to suffer social censure if they want to explore so-called 'feminine' traits, like motherliness or sensitivity.

In a nutshell
Hatred of women.

Why it matters
Misogyny is bad in itself and enforces sexist ideology.

Key figures
Gloria Anzaldúa, 1942–2004
Moya Bailey
Kristie Dotson, b.1975
Sabina Lovibond

Make the connection
racism, p.51
ideology, p.66
identity politics, p.90

prejudice

'I don't want a tomato, tomatoes are gross.'
'How do you know they're gross when you've never even tried one?'

You can be prejudiced against all sorts of things, from tomatoes to cities, from cars to flavours of ice cream. Strictly speaking, a prejudice is simply a prejudgement, a view or opinion of something that isn't based on actual experience of the thing.

Mostly when we're talking about prejudice, we're talking about judgements made about groups of people. These judgements are sometimes formed on the basis of characteristics such as race, gender and religion. All too often, we learn social stories about certain groups (stereotypes), then form judgements about group members without necessarily having met any of them. If people know that I'm Jewish, they might infer, based on negative stereotypes, that I'm part of a cliquey, globally powerful community (I'm not) – conspiracy theories like this one can emerge out of stereotypes.

Prejudice can manifest in both negative and seemingly positive ways. There are, for instance, stereotypes about Jewish people being funny and good at business. I might benefit from such prejudices in the short term (people may be primed to laugh at my jokes more readily), but even positive prejudices are damaging. A prejudice is careless reasoning, if it can be counted as reasoning at all, which includes the assumption that all members of a group are the same and unable to act independently, as individuals.

In a nutshell
A prejudgement, a view you arrive at before examining the relevant evidence.

Why it matters
As unreliable judgements, prejudices can lead to unsound arguments and discrimination.

Key figures
Linda Martín Alcoff
W. E. B. Du Bois, 1868–1963
Alicia Garza, b.1981
Gayatri Spivak, b.1942

Make the connection
privilege, p.40
race, p.42
oppression, p.52
double consciousness, p.136

racism

Racism is a specific form of prejudice. It involves the belief that some people are superior to others because of their race (the racist view that white people are superior to other groups is known as 'white supremacy'). Moreover, racism is a prejudice that is, on some level, socially endorsed. Racism is a prejudice supported by power.

When a student of colour scornfully makes fun of his white classmate by saying that she eats tasteless food and can't dance, this is a prejudice. It's a prejudice that focuses on race. However, while it may be hurtful it isn't racist, because society privileges and empowers white people more than people of colour. Racism is prejudice with social backing. When a white student says that her Black classmate must be an excellent dancer, she does so within the context of a society that routinely and systematically frames Black people as more 'physical' and less cerebral, one that celebrates athletic prowess over other achievements. This is a prejudice based on race, with social power, which makes it racism.

The term racism is complicated by the fact that race is a social, rather than a biological, classification. People can be 'raced' or 'racialized' (that is, seen to be a specific race) differently in different contexts. Sometimes, I'm raced as white. Sometimes I'm racialized as Jewish (this raises the question as to whether antisemitism is a racism or another kind of prejudice). Sometimes I'm racialized as 'Arab'. Race is a social construction, so society determines who is and isn't white and what privileges they are afforded as a result.

In a nutshell
Socially empowered prejudice, which focuses on race.

Why it matters
It is a form of oppression that needs to be identified in order to be combatted.

Key figures
Sara Ahmed, b.1969
Patricia Hill Collins, b.1948
Charles W. Mills, 1951–2021
Shirley Anne Tate, b.1956

Make the connection
privilege, p.40
race, p.42
capitalism, p.98
consciousness raising, p.137

oppression

Generally speaking, oppression is the unjust or cruel exercise of authority over individuals or groups. It is usually understood to emerge at the structural or institutional level, manifesting in legal, economic and political policies that impose unjust burdens on specific people.

We might, perhaps, talk about an individual being oppressive, but on the whole we tend to talk about oppressive regimes, oppressive environments and oppressive societies. It's big-picture stuff. Apartheid South Africa, which limited the political rights and restricted the movement of Black and brown South Africans, was an oppressive society. Nazi Germany and the Khmer Rouge are also examples of oppressive regimes. Many of us assume nowadays that we live in free societies, but governments are still engaged in oppressive policy decisions, whether it's because you're racially minoritized, transgender or a migrant.

Oppression often results from prejudices, including racism, and is indexed to characteristics such as race, gender, class, nationality and disability. Oppression is the concrete realization of these prejudices. For instance, many governments create what has been termed a 'hostile environment', with the aim of curbing immigration, by creating an explicitly hostile (oppressive) environment for undocumented immigrants. A series of policies, such as tighter visa rules and immigration checks on renters, create an unwelcoming climate to disincentivize immigration.

In a nutshell
The unjust or cruel exercise of authority over groups or individuals.

Why it matters
It is a form of injustice that characterizes many social relationships. We need to be aware of it in order to resist it.

Key figures
Anna Julia Cooper, 1858–1964
Paul Gilroy, b.1956
Charles W. Mills, 1951–2021
Iris Marion Young, 1949–2006

Make the connection
sexism, p.48
racism, p.51
neoliberalism, p.99

domination

While oppression can be faceless, 'domination' refers to a specific relationship between the powerful and the less powerful. It involves the restriction of the freedom and autonomy of one group to the benefit of another. This, at least, is how political theorist Iris Marion Young differentiates the two concepts. Domination emphasizes dynamics within social relationships; those who dominate have the ability to shape and control the actions, choices and opportunities of others (typically to their disadvantage).

Oppression can be spoken about in passive terms. An oppressive atmosphere does not necessarily require that there are people there doing the oppression (it might just refer to a really small and stuffy room). Domination, meanwhile, is active – or rather interactive – figuring in interpersonal interactions. One group *dominates* another group, imposing their will, their beliefs, their way of thinking. The word 'dominate' comes from the Latin *dominus*, meaning 'master', and a master is a master over others.

For Young, oppression is a systemic and largely group-based form of injustice, rooted in social structures and institutions. Domination is more about the exercise of power within social relationships. This need not be exclusively political. Within sport, for instance, one football team can be said to dominate another if they keep possession of the ball and score multiple goals. In the financial sphere, a particular tech giant can dominate the market, outperforming their competitors.

In a nutshell
An oppressive relationship between individuals or groups.

Why it matters
Some forms of domination are less serious than others; when domination is combined with oppression, the effects can be deeply, sometimes fatally, damaging.

Key figures
Gloria Anzaldúa, 1942–2004
Frantz Fanon, 1925–1961
Toussaint Louverture, 1797–1802
Sojourner Truth, c.1797–1883

Make the connection
racism, p.51
identity politics, p.90
capitalism, p.98

rote

Back when I was at school, many, many years ago, I learned my times tables by repeating them over and over. One times two is two, two times two is four ... This repetitious form of education is known as 'rote learning'. Rote learning is mechanical and sometimes performed without full understanding or engagement. I was also encouraged to learn Shakespeare 'by heart', which involved a lot of repetition, but considerably less understanding of the arcane phrasing (what exactly is a 'mortal coil'?). The point of rote learning is to create mental stores of information, which can be accessed and understood at a later date.

According to virtue ethicists, we can develop positive character traits through a similar process. If you think kindness is an important virtue, the virtue ethicist might encourage you to repeatedly perform kind acts until they become second nature, i.e., a spontaneous response ingrained in your character rather than the product of deliberation. Just as I can tell you, unthinkingly, that eight times eight equals sixty-four, someone who has practised kindness over and over and over again can, unthinkingly, perform kind acts. Virtue ethicists call this process 'habituation'. It's a matter of cultivating virtuous habits through rote learning. As with mathematics or poetry, this kind of moral education is most effective when the student is engaged and understands what's going on.

In a nutshell
Rote learning is a form of learning, used in academic and (sometimes) ethical spheres.

Why it matters
Ethical rote learning offers a different perspective on ethical decision-making, emphasizing the honing of ethical instincts rather than rational deliberation.

Key figures
Pierre Bourdieu, 1930–2002
Confucius, c.551–479 BCE
Martha Nussbaum, b.1947

Make the connection
empathy, p.26
instinct, p.34
ethics, p.39
being good, p.45

rite

When you do something by rote, you do it over and over again. It's a practice, involving repeated performances (of kindness or courage, for example). In this sense, there's some overlap with rituals and rites. A rite is a formal ceremony, a performance often regularly repeated. A Catholic mass is a rite, as is the Friday night Shabbat service, and the Islamic call to prayer. These are performances that people conduct over and over, with, on some level, the same aim as rote learning: to cultivate a virtuous character.

In some Classical Chinese philosophy, rites are seen to be a fundamental part of ethical and social life. Within Confucian thought, for example, they are significant not just as a way to cultivate virtuous character (to tone your ethical muscles), but in and of themselves. By engaging in rites and rituals, individuals can demonstrate their understanding of social relationships. Rites allow citizens to better comprehend their roles – e.g., what it means to be a good son or a good father – and in so doing, contribute to social order and harmony.

Of course, while social harmony can be desirable, some societies are profoundly regressive – and 'harmony' may have the net result that some people benefit at the expense of others. Many social rites, both secular and religious, reinforce roles that position men at the top of the hierarchy, above everyone else. The wedding rite is a classic example, in which the bride's father 'gives away' his daughter, as though she was once his property and has become her husband's.

In a nutshell
A social ceremony, either religious (e.g., a baptism) or secular (e.g., a prom).

Why it matters
These shared activities often dictate what is and isn't socially acceptable or desirable.

Key figures
Sara Ahmed, b.1969
Gloria Anzaldúa, 1942–2004
Clare Chambers, b.1976
Kate Manne, b.1983

Make the connection
ethics, p.39
privilege, p.40
hegemony, p.67

scepticism

When a student tells her teacher that the dog ate her homework, the teacher may raise an eyebrow. 'Really?' she may say. 'I doubt that very much.' That's scepticism. It's a questioning, doubtful attitude to something you've been told. In epistemology, the study of knowledge, it involves questioning the reliability of knowledge claims. Sceptics (or 'skeptics', depending on where you live) are cautious folk who encourage a critical approach to supposed truths and emphasize a need for careful reasoning and robust evidence. Doubt, including 'radical doubt', is their favourite argumentative tool, or 'heuristic device'.

But sceptics aren't just doubters, they're inquirers too. The term comes from the Greek word *skepsis*, which means 'inquiry' or 'examination'. The sceptic's approach is to raise an eyebrow and then say, 'Tell me more.' They don't just doubt everything willy-nilly. They doubt with the aim of finding secure foundations; the intention is to discard unwarranted assumptions in the search for truth. The teacher doesn't have any evidence that the student's dog really *did* eat her homework, but all the empirical evidence suggests that (whether or not it was completed) there is no homework on the student's desk.

The sceptic isn't necessarily averse to conjecture. The teacher can consider the student's story and ask for more information (and continue to raise an eyebrow as it's supplied). They may ultimately be persuaded – if, for instance, the student shows them a video of the dog eating her homework – but the sceptic is hard to convince.

In a nutshell
A questioning, doubtful attitude.

Why it matters
There's a lot of misinformation about (on the internet, among other places), and scepticism will help you avoid being duped.

Key figures
Elisabeth of Bohemia, 1618–1680
René Descartes, 1596–1650
Sextus Empiricus, c.300–200 BCE

Make the connection

suspicion

A sceptical approach can be useful, but it's good manners, sometimes at least, to give people the benefit of the doubt. Dialogue can be difficult enough without an interlocutor constantly questioning your knowledge claims ('Yes, but how can you say that for *sure?*'). If you're having an argument, philosophical or otherwise, the best way to resolve it isn't necessarily unremitting scepticism. Not only can constant questioning prevent progress, it may undermine the good will of whoever is engaging in dialogue. It's just not *polite*.

The 'hermeneutics of suspicion' is an interpretative approach that doubles down on the sceptic's doubt (hermeneutics is the study of interpretation). Scepticism is a general doubt; suspicion, in this context, is the idea that someone is actively trying to pull the wool over your eyes. While the sceptic may interpret a knowledge claim as a lazy assumption, the suspicious person might read it as an agenda.

When someone says, for instance, that unremitting scepticism is impolite and bad manners, the suspicious person will wonder, 'What exactly are they trying to hide?' Conventions about what is and isn't polite are constructed in specific cultural contexts and, the suspicious person might say, they may well be designed to stop people asking questions. We're told that it's poor form to talk about politics (along with sex and religion), but who stands to benefit from this? Disincentivizing political engagement serves people who are already in power. Suspicion, like scepticism, can be an important and insightful interpretative tool.

In a nutshell
An active, wary scepticism.

Why it matters
Oppressive systems can be pervasive, so it's best to be on your guard (epistemically speaking).

Key figures
Nora Berenstain
Darren Chetty, b.1972
Audre Lorde, 1934–1992
Jacques Rancière, b.1940

Make the connection
knowledge, p.8
semantics, p.122
'philosophy', p.154

qualitative identity

I once knew someone who worked as a quality controller in a chocolate factory. Every day he was asked to assess the quality of the chocolates and make sure they were up to scratch. This is an (especially delicious) example of 'qualitative' assessment.

In the case of a chocolate taster, the qualities being assessed are things like texture, aroma and sweetness. These are the distinctive features that quality controllers are supposed to keep an eye (or tongue) on, to make sure they don't change. Raspberry truffles are always supposed to taste like raspberries.

Does a chocolate taster assess whether qualities are *indistinguishable* or *identical*? The first requires a sophisticated palate and falls properly within the remit of quality control. Qualitative *identity*, however, requires metaphysical analysis. What does it mean when we say that one truffle tastes the *same* as another truffle? Some metaphysicians argue that the sameness in taste can be explained by reference to abstract objects called 'universals'. When you imagine the sound of fingernails on a chalkboard, you gain access to a specific (and specifically unpleasant) universal. It's in relation to these universals that we can say one taste is the same as another.

Other metaphysicians, called 'nominalists', are less keen on the idea of free-floating universal entities. They argue that qualities only exist in material things. There is no Raspberry-Truffleness, only lots of raspberry truffles. Nominalists avoid invoking abstract entities, but it's harder for them to explain what makes two walnut pralines taste the same.

In a nutshell
Qualitative relates to the quality of something. Qualitative identity refers to one thing being the same quality as another.

Why it matters
Being able to pick out and discuss qualities (and the substances that possess them) is fundamental to our understanding of the world.

Key figures
Ruth Barcan Marcus, 1921–2012
Gottfried Wilhelm Leibniz, 1646–1716
John Locke, 1632–1704
A. N. Whitehead, 1861–1947

Make the connection
identity, p.6
essential, p.62
substratum, p.82

QUALITY CONTROL

quantitative identity

In contrast to qualitative identity, quantitative identity relates to (drum roll, please) *quantity*. If I told you my friend ate on average one hundred chocolates a day, that would be a quantitative assessment. If I said he ate the same number of chocolates every day, I would be making a claim about quantitative identity. The number of chocolates he ate on one day is identical to the number of chocolates he ate on another.

It seems that if we're making a claim about qualitative identity, we're also making a claim about quantitative identity. So, do the two types of identity ever diverge from one another? In matters of personal identity, we might perhaps argue that qualities can change while quantitative identity is preserved. When my friend started working at the chocolate factory, he was much younger than he is now. These days he is taller and has fewer teeth. He is a father and a husband and a black belt in karate. In qualitative terms, he is very different from the man who started at the chocolate factory so many years ago. But he's the same person; his quantitative identity over time has remained the same. He hasn't split into two or three or four; he is the same one person (and, surprisingly enough, he is still a massive fan of chocolates).

In a nutshell
Quantitative relates to quantity: how much or how many of a given thing there are. Quantitative identity relates to the sameness of quantity.

Why it matters
Our ability to grasp quantity and quantitative identity allows us to navigate the world.

Key figures
Plutarch, c.49–119 CE
Lynne Rudder Baker, 1944–2017
David Wiggins, b.1933

Make the connection
identity, p.6
deduction, p.61
existence, p.70

induction

The word 'induction' can be used in lots of different ways. You have induction days at university, when you're shown around and told what's what. In the context of childbirth, labour can be induced (prompted by drugs, when it doesn't happen naturally). When I was growing up, I had an induction heater in my bedroom, which relied on an electromagnetic process (induction) to generate heat. The word comes from the Latin *inducere*, which is where we get the word 'duct' from; induction is a path, a passage into something.

In philosophical logic, induction refers to a form of reasoning that involves deriving general principles or conclusions from specific observations. Take, for example, a naturalist and her study of swans. This naturalist, who works in a specific region in the northern hemisphere, has been observing swans for decades and has consistently found them to have white feathers. She has made several individual observations that, collectively, encourage her to make the general claim that *all* swans are white.

Inductive reasoning moves from particular observations or claims to more general ones. As such, it's fallible. A single counter-example could disprove the general statement. The claim that all swans are white is based on a restricted evidence base and, in fact, black swans are common in southeast and southwest Australia and Tasmania.

Inductive reasoning is a type of inference. It involves the process of deriving conclusions based on the available (if sometimes insufficient) evidence. It is not, however, the only type of inferential reasoning.

In a nutshell
Inductive reasoning involves deriving general principles from individual observations or claims.

Why it matters
Inductive reasoning is central to much of scientific practice (and many other forms of reasoning too).

Key figures
Francis Bacon, 1561–1626
Nancy Cartwright, b.1944
Helen Longino, b.1944
Evelyn Fox Keller, 1936–2023

Make the connection
imply, p.10
a posteriori, p.81
conjunction, p.116

All swans are white.

deduction

'Deduction' doesn't have quite as many conflicting meanings as 'induction'. There aren't (as far as I know) deduction heaters, deduced births or deduction days at universities. Deduction almost always refers to the form of inferential reasoning that involves deriving specific conclusions from general principles. While inductive reasoning is bottom-up, deductive reasoning is top-down. For example, based on the (plausible) general claim that all humans are mortal, and the (hopefully plausible) claim that I am a human, you can reach the specific conclusion that I am mortal.

Deductive reasoning is more rigid and deterministic than induction. The truth of the conclusion is supposed to be guaranteed if the premises are true. If the premises are true, it can't later be discovered (after further investigation) that I'm actually a robot.

If you're solving a crime and want your case to stand up in court, deductive reasoning seems to be the preferred choice. Detectives don't want to generate general principles – for example, that all fraudsters have blonde hair. Rather, the aim is to reach a specific conclusion. If internet fraud requires access to the internet and the only suspect who had such access was Alan, then we can deduce that Alan was the internet fraudster.

While induced conclusions are probable and contain a degree of uncertainty, deduced conclusions are certain if the premises are true. Induction, then, is a more flexible form of reasoning, since it allows for the revision of conclusions based on new observations.

In a nutshell
If you deduce something, you derive a conclusion about something specific from more general principles or premises.

Why it matters
Deduction is one of the many ways we work out puzzles.

Key figures
G. E. M. Anscombe, 1919–2001
Nancy Cartwright, b.1944
Valerie Gray Hardcastle

Make the connection
infer, p.11
contradiction, p.64
a priori, p.80

I deduce it's you!

essential

Apples are an essential ingredient for apple pie. No brainer. It's part of the definition of apple pie that it contains apples. Here, the term 'essential' refers to a constituent part that is crucial, indispensable or otherwise fundamental to the nature or identity of a thing.

It's an essential property of squares that they have four sides and of triangles that they have three. If a square ceases to have four sides it is no longer a square, and if a triangle gains two sides it's no longer a triangle. Similarly, it's part of the essence of human being that we are cordates (we have hearts). You are a human (I assume), so you have a heart.

What else is essential to you? There are a few physiological things we can call 'essential', but you might also think you have essential character traits. Would you be *you* if you weren't the witty and charismatic intellectual currently reading this book? Maybe. Presumably you weren't always witty. It's unlikely you were cracking jokes when you were a newly born baby. It's not always easy to work out what is and isn't an essential property.

Think again about your humanness. It is, supposedly, part of the essence of humans to be cordates. But what if you have your human heart removed and someone else's fitted? Does it still count as a heart, albeit a mechanical one, or has something more fundamental changed? Your view of what is and isn't essential will affect when you think something might cease to exist.

In a nutshell
The essence of what something is relates to how we think of it 'in a nutshell'.

Why it matters
Our view of an object's essence determines when we think it comes into existence and ceases to exist.

Key figures
Donna Haraway, b.1944
N. Katherine Hayles, b.1943
Luce Irigaray, b.1930
David Wiggins, b.1933

Make the connection
existence, p.70
a priori, p.80
ontology, p.114

100% apple pie

intrinsic

The term 'intrinsic' is conceptually tied to the notion of an essence, but they're not quite the same. An intrinsic property or attribute is inherent or integral to something. An intrinsic property is part of what that something *is*. So, for example, the mass of an object is an intrinsic property. The same is true for its density and chemical composition.

Intrinsic properties are typically contrasted with extrinsic ones. While intrinsic properties are part of what an object is, extrinsic properties depend on external factors or relationships with other entities. The value of a nugget of gold is an extrinsic property (since the value is dependent on human views about which metals are valuable and which aren't). Location is another extrinsic property. Describing someone in a photograph as being 'on the left' of someone else is a description of an extrinsic property.

A lot of the time, intrinsic properties overlap with essential properties. It's an intrinsic property of water that it is constituted by hydrogen and oxygen molecules. It is also part of the definition (the essence) of water that it has this chemical composition. However, while the loss of an essential property constitutes the end of an object, the same isn't necessarily true for the removal of an intrinsic property. I currently weigh 11 stone, and this weight is an intrinsic property, but I could become heavier or lighter. Weighing 11 stone isn't essential to me.

In a nutshell
Intrinsic properties are ones that are inherent or integral to an object. Unlike essential properties, however, they aren't necessary for an entity's continued existence.

Why it matters
Being able to distinguish intrinsic from extrinsic properties helps us assess, for example, an object's value.

Key figures
Saul Kripke, 1940–2022
Jennifer Nagel
Hilary Putnam, 1926–2016
Charlotte Witt, b.1951

Make the connection

contradiction

'Why are you looking at me like that?'
'I'm not looking at you like that!'

Contradiction comes from the Latin *contra*, meaning 'against',
and *dicere*, meaning 'to speak'; to contradict is to speak against
someone. It's the stuff all good arguments are made from.

In logic, a contradiction is a conflict between two or more
propositions. Logical contradictions don't need to be voiced by
different parties. They can exist in the same statement. If you say,
'My friend is faultless despite their faults', you have asserted two
things which are in direct opposition. Either your friend is faultless,
in which case they don't have faults, or they have faults, in which
case they aren't faultless.

Being faultless despite one's faults is a contradiction in terms.
Other such contradictions include the encouragement to act
naturally (acting is intentional behaviour and therefore not natural),
and the notion of 'a resounding silence' (silence, by definition, is the
absence of sound).

In formal logic, contradictions are pitfalls that logicians want to
avoid. A foundational principle in classical logic is the Law of
Non-Contradiction, which is essentially: don't contradict yourself!
However, contradictions can also be useful to logicians. The truth
of a proposition can be demonstrated if you can reliably show that
its negation leads to a contradiction.

In a nutshell
A contradiction is a
logical inconsistency.

Why it matters
Contradiction, and
self-contradiction,
can fatally undermine
an argument.

Key figures
Gottlob Frege,
1848–1925
Sandra Harding, b.1935
Penelope Maddy,
b.1950
Ludwig Wittgenstein,
1889–1951

Make the connection

paradox

'This sentence is a lie.' As statements go, this is one of the weirder ones. If the sentence *is* a lie, then it's true ... in which case it *isn't* a lie ... in which case it's true ... The mental revolutions leave you reeling.

A paradox is a special kind of contradiction. The Liar's Paradox, described above, relies on a conflict between the truth and falsity of that sentence. But a paradox is more than a contradiction. Some contradictions can be resolved relatively easily – if, for example, one of the propositions is obviously false. Were I to say, 'I have a beard and I don't have a beard', one of these propositions can be proved (by examining my chin). The Liar's Paradox, by contrast, refers to itself. There is no recourse to external evidence.

Moreover, paradoxes aren't just logical problems to be overcome. They often invite further reflection. The word 'paradox' refers to the Greek concept of *doxa*, which means (very roughly) a set of beliefs and practices. Doxa are ingrained assumptions that shape the way we see the world. The Greek work *para* means 'contrary to' or 'beyond', so a paradox is a conceptual device that might push you beyond your everyday worldview. The Liar's Paradox has been written about endlessly and causes us to question both the notions of true and false, and the Law of Non-Contradiction itself.

A contradiction involves a direct and explicit conflict between statements, but a paradox is a contradiction with an edge, one that may help reframe our understanding of long-held beliefs or assumptions.

In a nutshell
A paradox is a logical contradiction that can lead to further reflection.

Why it matters
Paradoxes point to the gaps in our understanding or peculiarities with the way we think of the world.

Key figures
Al-Ghazali, c.1058–1111 CE
Pierre Bourdieu, 1930–2002
Ibn Sina, 'Avicenna', c.980–1037
Graham Priest, b.1948

Make the connection

ideology

Ideology is the background set of beliefs, values and ideas that shape the thinking of an individual or (more usually) a group of individuals. Typically, these beliefs relate to politics, society and culture. An ideology provides a framework for understanding the world.

You can think of it a bit like a map. There are, for instance, lots of different maps of London. There is the London Undergound (or 'Tube') map and the Overground map. There are printed maps, which have all the road names and landmarks, and there's Google Maps too. Each one gives you a different perspective on London, accenting the way you might navigate the city. A 'Tube' map assumes that you travel on the Tube. Google Maps assumes that you are computer literate. Just as different maps prioritize different routes to the same place, different ideologies prioritize different beliefs, values and methods (often to reach the same goal, such as peace).

Ideology affects every aspect of society and is, therefore, quite hard to spot. It's easier to see if you don't share the same ideological assumptions as everyone else. In the US, for example, there's an assumption that a happy life involves marriage, home ownership and children. This ideology is felt most keenly by people who are excluded from it, by those who aren't married, don't own homes and aren't interested in having kids. These people can understand the way a 'nuclear family' can benefit others because they themselves receive dis-benefits through their failure to conform.

In a nutshell
A specific set of background beliefs and values.

Why it matters
Ideology permeates everything, often very subtly. It can have negative effects, which we only recognize once it's too late.

Key figures
Stuart Hall, 1932–2014
Sophie Lewis, b.1988
Rosa Luxembourg, 1871–1919
Karl Marx, 1818–1883

Make the connection
intuition, p.35
privilege, p.40
sexism, p.48

monogamy   home ownership   car

LIFE MAP

savings   nuclear family

university   work

hegemony

Ideology refers to diverse belief systems that can be shared across groups. Hegemony is more specific. The term, which comes from the Greek *hegemonia*, meaning 'supremacy' or 'leadership', refers to the dominance of one group over another, where the dominant group shapes social beliefs and values (i.e., it enforces ideological assumptions) for its own benefit.

Think about the English aristocracy, a powerful social class in which members hold titles such as duke, earl and baron. For centuries, the aristocracy have set social standards and expectations that exclude people from the 'lower classes'. If you're a lord, for example, you may be given access to the House of Lords, a powerful arm of the British government. Moreover, it is only by conforming to the etiquette set by the aristocracy – and in which the aristocracy are well trained – that people are given access to 'polite society' (which really means 'powerful society'). Failure to understand the correct manners can, in certain circles, lead to social censure.

Hegemony is a form of ideological manipulation that operates primarily through culture. It is less overt than military control and considerably easier, too. It doesn't require overt violence. It involves coercion and subtle forms of influencing through cultural products such as films or books (think of all the TV series, such as *Bridgerton* and *The Crown*, which feature romances within the nobility and the obsession with the British monarchy). As such, it can be even harder to combat.

In a nutshell
The supremacist ideology of a dominant group.

Why it matters
Hegemonic forces are oppressive and shape our day-to-day lives.

Key figures
Angela Davis, b.1944
Alicia Garza, b.1981
Antonio Gramsci, 1891–1937
Charles W. Mills, 1951–2021

Make the connection
liberalism, p.47
oppression, p.52
poststructuralism, p.111

empiricism

While the adjectives 'empirical' and 'rational' appear to overlap (a scientific inquiry could be both), empiricism and rationalism are intellectual movements usually positioned in opposition. They refer to contrasting philosophical views about the sources and nature of knowledge.

The word 'empiricism' comes from the Greek *empeiria*, meaning 'experience'. Empiricists hold that knowledge is primarily derived from our lived engagement with the world. According to empiricists, all of our ideas are based on things we have seen or heard or otherwise encountered. Your idea of an eagle, for instance, is based on having seen an eagle or having read about them. Your idea of a lion is the result of you having seen a lion or (more likely) seen a photograph of one. The idea of a griffin, a mythical beast that has the body of a lion and the head of an eagle, is a combination of your ideas about eagles and lions. There's nothing in the mind that you didn't first, in some way, experience.

Empiricists have a particular 'philosophy of mind', which is to say they think the mind works in a specific way. Since they believe that knowledge is acquired primarily (and perhaps exclusively) through experience, they hold that we are born with our heads empty. The mind is a *tabula rasa* (Latin for 'blank slate') on which ideas based on experience are imprinted.

Empiricists tend to privilege science as a way of generating knowledge. Empirical evidence is gathered and, through inductive reasoning, general claims are made.

In a nutshell
An approach to inquiry that privileges experience over abstract theorizing.

Why it matters
Despite emerging from seventeenth-century philosophical trends, empiricism remains one of the most popular forms of scientific inquiry today.

Key figures
Robert Boyle, 1627–1691
Margaret Cavendish, 1623–1673
David Hume, 1711–1776
John Locke, 1632–1704

Make the connection
induction, p.60
a posteriori, p.81
materialism, p.124

rationalism

If empiricists privilege science, then rationalists might be said to privilege mathematics and logic. You don't work out equations through scientific investigation. The number two isn't something you can find in the wild and put under a microscope. The rationalist believes that knowledge can be acquired without sensory experience. Scientific inquiry may be helpful, but fundamental truths are apprehended through reason alone.

Where the empiricists think we arrive in the world with empty heads, the rationalist argues that there are innate ideas, i.e. ideas we are born with. There are some things we know without having to consult the external world, including (they argue) mathematical truths. Consequently, where empiricism primarily relies on inductive reasoning, rationalism is associated with deduction. Innate principles are drawn on to reach specific conclusions. It might be argued that we have an innate understanding of addition. It's because of this that any one of us can, theoretically, deduce that $2 + 2 = 4$ and $4 + 4 = 8$.

Of course, these explanations of rationalism and empiricism, as with all 'isms', involve unhelpful generalization. The terms are applied to thinkers (primarily working in the sixteenth and seventeenth centuries), but they identify trends and tendencies rather than hard-and-fast doctrines. While they're typically placed in opposition, many scholars of the time and since have acknowledged that the two methods could, in some areas, complement each other.

In a nutshell
Involves a focus on rationality as the means by which we can understand the fundamental truths of reality.

Why it matters
Like empiricism, rationalism is (in some sense at least) still very popular.

Key figures
Anton Wilhelm Amo, 1703–1759
Nancy Cartwright, b.1944
Evelyn Fox Keller, 1936–2023
Linda Zagzebski, b.1946

Make the connection
deduction, p.61
scientific, p.96
know–that, p.109

existence

What is existence? On one level, it's simply the state of being real. Objects exist when they're actually *there* in the world. I exist (I promise) and you exist (I hope), and the book that you're reading exists, because otherwise what would you be reading? Unicorns *don't* exist. Nor do elves or fairies or hobgoblins.

Mythical beasts don't appear to exist. They're just the product of our imaginations. But if they're products, maybe in some sense they *do* exist. Perhaps different things exist in different ways? Think about the words you're reading. Do they exist? I would say that they do. If they didn't, there wouldn't be much point in me writing this sentence. But *how* do they exist? The word 'exist' exists, but is it just a collection of marks on a page, or sounds produced by someone's mouth? And what about numbers? Does the number two exist? If it doesn't, why does it conform to such strict laws? If you divide two by two, you get one. These laws are independent of human minds.

Metaphysics is the area of philosophy that examines existence, and different metaphysical traditions have different answers to questions about what exists and how. What seems, at first, relatively straightforward is in fact rather complicated. Do fictional characters like Sherlock Holmes exist? And what about impossible objects like round squares, or immaterial substances like souls and angels, to say nothing of God?

In a nutshell
The state of being real.

Why it matters
Our engagement with the world is premised on our understanding of what does and doesn't exist. Gravity exists; dragons, not so much.

Key figures
Aristotle,
c.384–322 BCE
Sandra Harding, b.1935
Martin Heidegger,
1889–1976
Amie Thomasson,
b.1968

Make the connection

subsistence

Metaphysicians have come up with a bunch of terms to separate out the different modes of being, and 'subsistence' is one of these.

Subsistence has a broader remit than existence and describes an abstract level of being. All existing things, like the book you're reading, subsist, but other things subsist without existing in actuality. They're not 'externally real', but they're still around. A number is an example of an object with 'mere' subsistence. There are other objects, too, which are sometimes said to have 'non-being'. These objects don't subsist at all and can be split into two categories: contradictory objects, like a round square, or non-contradictory objects, like a perpetual-motion machine.

To make matters more perplexing, metaphysicians have terms to describe different modes of continued existence. How do existing objects *continue* to exist, i.e., to survive? Some think that things – like you and me – 'endure'. We persist as whole objects, wholly present at each moment of our existence. Others think that we 'perdure'. Perdurantists believe that we have 'temporal parts', such as 'you-as-a-baby' and 'you-as-a-toddler', in the same way that we have spatial parts (e.g., a left arm, a right leg). You don't move as a single, complete object *through* time. Rather, you are spread out *over* time.

'Existence' is a broad term that can be used to capture different types of being. 'Subsistence', 'endurance' and 'perdurance' are more precise terms, used to clarify an object's mode of being.

In a nutshell
A way of being.

Why it matters
Understanding degrees of existence, like subsistence or perdurance, allows us to more precisely understand the warp and weft of reality.

Key figures
Sally Haslanger, b.1955
David Lewis, 1941–2001
Alexius Meinong, 1853–1920
Plato, *c*.428–423 BCE

Make the connection
contradiction, p.64
phenomenology, p.118
physicalism, p.125

You're a real idea.

validity

In daily life, when we describe something as valid or invalid, we're normally referring to its legitimacy. 'Is that coupon still valid?' 'No, it went out of date three years ago.' In logical life, 'validity' has a similar, but more specific meaning. It refers to the formal structure of an argument. An argument is considered valid if the conclusion follows logically from the premises (i.e., the conclusion must be true if the premises are true).

If an argument is valid, it will never go out of date. Validity is independent of the actual truth or falsity of the premises and conclusion. To say that an argument is valid is simply to assess whether or not it abides by the laws of logic. A valid argument structure ensures that *if* the premises are true, then the conclusion is true. It doesn't require that the premises are in fact true. For example, you might want to argue that Charles III is actually an alien. Such an argument could run as follows:

Premise 1:   All members of the royal family are aliens.

Premise 2:   Charles III is a member of the royal family.

Conclusion: Charles III is an alien.

You would be perfectly within your rights to deny that all members of the royal family are aliens. The argument itself, however, is still valid. It obeys the laws of logic. *If* the premises are true, *then* the king really is an alien.

In a nutshell
If an argument is valid, it abides by the laws of logic.

Why it matters
If an argument is invalid, you shouldn't be persuaded by it.

Key figures
Dorothy Edgington, b.1941
Gottlob Frege, 1848–1925
Gillian Russell
Linda Zagzebski, b.1946

Make the connection

valid premise =
valid conclusion

soundness

'Sound' can mean 'road worthy', 'reliable' or 'competent'. In logic, however, soundness refers to the truth value of an argument's premises. An argument is sound if it's valid *and* all of its premises are true. Not only must the conclusion follow logically from the premises, but the premises (and therefore the conclusion) must be true as well. A sound argument might run as follows:

Premise 1: All members of the royal family are related to Charles III by blood or marriage.

Premise 2: Prince Harry is a member of the royal family.

Conclusion: Prince Harry is related to Charles III by blood or marriage.

This argument is sound. Prince Harry is indeed related to Charles III.

The difference between validity and soundness can be helpful in finding points of agreements between opposing positions. By differentiating between the two, interlocutors can pinpoint where exactly they disagree. They might agree that an argument is valid, but if one of the premises is in dispute, they can disagree that the argument is sound. If you have evidence that Prince Harry is someone else's son, you can question the soundness of the argument above. If you have categorical proof that Charles III has tentacles and a spaceship, you might think he's an alien after all.

In a nutshell
An argument is sound if it is valid and its premises are true.

Why it matters
Understanding whether an argument is sound will affect whether or not we find it persuasive.

Key figures
Ruth Barcan Marcus, 1921–2012
Alfred Tarski, 1901–1983
David Wiggins, b.1933
Ludwig Wittgenstein, 1889–1951

Make the connection
induction, p.60
contradiction, p.64
conjunction, p.116

true premise
+ valid conclusion
= sound argument

prescriptive

When you go to the doctor and she decides you need antibiotics, she will probably write you a prescription. She says you need them and instructs you when and how to take them.

Prescriptive morality works in a similar way. Sometimes called 'normative morality', its advocates are concerned with providing behavioural guidelines. If you want to be a good person, a prescriptivist will be all too happy to issue directions (written or otherwise) to tell you which actions are morally right and which are morally wrong. (It's important not to confuse the term 'prescriptive' with 'proscriptive', which means that something is actively forbidden or 'proscribed'.)

Prescriptive moral theories tend to emphasize moral principles or codes of conduct that individuals and societies should follow. 'Do not lie', 'Do not steal', 'Do not murder'. These actions are wrong, and if you want to be moral, the thought goes, you must avoid doing them.

Consequentialist ethics, which evaluates the morality of actions based on their outcomes, is one of the most common types of prescriptive morality. Another is deontological ethics, which asserts that certain actions are inherently wrong, regardless of their consequences. Deontologists are like doctors who think you have to follow their instructions to the letter. Swallow pills with food at precisely midday or something dreadful will happen; always tell the truth or you will have committed an irredeemably immoral act.

In a nutshell
Prescriptive morality provides behavioural guidelines, principles and rules.

Why it matters
Prescriptive theories offer apparently clear instructions for how to live (e.g., the Ten Commandments).

Key figures
Augustine,
c.354–430 CE
Immanuel Kant,
1724–1804
Christine Korsgaard,
b.1952
Ban Zhao, c.35–100 CE

Make the connection
morality, p.38
doing good, p.44
normative, p.135

Be kind to others.

descriptive

As you might expect, descriptive morality involves *describing* pre-existing moral beliefs. The descriptivist looks to the world, to the behaviours of individuals and societies, in order to understand and answer moral questions. Descriptivists focus on the way we see ourselves behaving morally, then they codify these behaviours into moral systems.

As such, descriptive moral inquiries typically involve empirical research, like sociological studies. In this way, descriptivists gain insights into the different values held by different cultures and communities. The aim is to provide a clear (and hopefully objective) account of the moral landscape as it actually exists.

Moral relativism is a descriptive approach to morality. For relativists, moral values vary across culture. For example, in some countries, euthanasia – assisted suicide – is understood to be morally acceptable in certain situations, while in others it is strictly prohibited (on putatively moral grounds). A descriptive approach describes how different moral systems can form conflicting moral judgements.

Prescriptive morality is concerned with providing guidelines for moral behaviour, while descriptive morality focuses on describing and understanding actual moral practices that exist in different societies. Your approach to morality may include elements of both; you may think that there are some robust moral rules ('don't murder'), while also benefitting from an appreciation of how different cultures might weight murder differently in different circumstances (e.g., in cold blood or in war).

In a nutshell
Descriptive morality describes moral systems as they are found in the world.

Why it matters
Descriptivists are aware that the universalizing tendencies of the prescriptivists may come across as a bit bossy.

Key figures
Kwame Anthony Appiah, b.1954
Emmanuel Levinas, 1906–1995
Alasdair MacIntyre, b.1929
Martha Nussbaum, b.1947

Make the connection
liberal, p.46
subjective, p.76
normal, p.134

How often are you kind to others?

Research Department

subjective

Imagine you've just emerged from the cinema with one of your friends. 'That. Was. The. Greatest,' your friend announces. 'Best. Film. *Ever*.' You stare at them, nonplussed (and not just because of the odd way they're punctuating their sentences). 'You're kidding, right?' you say. 'That was the worst film I've ever seen.' 'Whatever!' your friend replies. 'That's just your opinion, okay?'

Opinions are subjective. They describe how you, as an individual, feel about something – in this case, a film. Beauty, taste and emotions are typically considered to be subjective because assessment of these things depends on the point of view of a *subject*. Relatedly, some people use 'subjective' to refer to the inner mental realm – an individual's perceptions, thoughts and experiences.

The truth of a subjective statement depends on the individual and their assessment of value. As such, these statements are very difficult to verify. Neuroscience has made some spectacular advances in recent years, but so far no one has come up with a way to feel someone else's feelings.

Recognizing whether or not a statement is subjective can be key to solving disagreements. Your conversation with your friend might go in one of two ways: either you might recognize that you have different tastes, or you might both emphatically declare the other wrong – and a lot of time and effort will be spent arguing and trying to change opinions. 'It's just *objectively bad*,' you might say (much to your friend's annoyance).

In a nutshell
Relates to an individual subject's position.

Why it matters
We don't always see eye to eye on everything. It's important to be able to distinguish subjective and objective claims in order to get along better.

Key figures
Gloria Anzaldúa, 1942–2004
Uma Narayan, b.1958
Edward Said, 1935–2003
Gayatri Spivak, b.1942

Make the connection
relativism, p.107
normal, p.134
'philosophy', p.154

objective

The term 'objective' refers to facts that are independent of personal preferences or interpretations. Objective statements aim to be impartial and verifiable, to capture reality and truth. The world as it really is. Scientific statements aim to be objective. It is an objective fact, for instance, that water boils at 100 degrees Celsius in the earth's atmosphere (calling it an 'objective fact' is almost tautological, since if something's a fact, it's supposed to be true of the world).

Scientific facts and mathematical truths are usually considered objective because they are independent of individual viewpoints. They capture 'objective reality', which is also the ambition of metaphysics. When materialists say that only matter (particles, etc.) exists, they are not making a subjective claim. They're saying this is true of the world. It's objective.

As American historian Lorraine Daston has noted, there are certain problems with claims to objectivity. Time and again in the history of science (and philosophy ... and pretty much everything), folk have claimed to describe objective reality when in fact they're only capturing local opinion. Statements like 'the sun revolves around the earth' and 'masturbation is immoral' have, at various times, been considered objective truths. But (spoiler alert) they're not. Positioning them as objective can be a rhetorical device to emphasize how fervently you believe. Unfortunately, this move can be used to disenfranchise certain groups. If you claim that scientific studies show that men are *objectively* more rational than women, then this will obviously impact how women are treated in society.

In a nutshell
Relates to a clear and neutral understanding of reality.

Why it matters
Objectivity is increasingly hard to come by, and increasingly important (not least in the media).

Key figures
Lorraine Daston, b.1951
Emmanuel Chukwudi Eze, 1963–2007
Sylvia Wynter, b.1928

Make the connection
knowledge, p.8
existence, p.70
ontology, p.114

accidental

'Sorry I stepped on your toe, it was an accident!' An accident is an unintentional action. To do something accidentally is to act without the intention to do so. That, anyway, is how we use 'accidental' in our day-to-day lives, to explain the broken vase, the tea that should have been coffee, and which certainly shouldn't have been spilled over your mother-in-law's lap.

In philosophy, the term 'accidental' has a related but slightly different meaning. It is used to describe something that isn't essential or necessary. In the academic literature, this usually means properties that aren't inherent to the objects that have them. Consider, for instance, this book. The text you're reading is made up of black letters on a white page. But these properties – the colours – are accidental to the book. The book would still be a book if the letters were blue and the page was orange (though it might be harder to read). Meanwhile, if you took the pages out, or deleted the text and images, you could argue that the book had ceased to be a book.

What does and doesn't count as essential – or accidental – is frequently up for debate. You might claim, for instance, that pagination is an essential property of books. It is an essential, rather than an accidental, property. But what about eBooks? If they're accessed through a screen, can they strictly speaking be said to have pages? And if not, are they not really, truly books?

In a nutshell
Accidental properties are ones that are dependent on extrinsic factors.

Why it matters
Recognizing accidents helps us get a surer grip on the deeper nature and character of the entities we encounter.

Key figures
Donna Haraway, b.1944
Saul Kripke, 1940–2022
Bertrand Russell, 1872–1970

Make the connection
essential, p.62
substratum, p.82
intention, p.128

There are no words. Is it still a book?

contingent

Contingency refers to a state of being that is dependent on certain conditions and could have been otherwise. A statement is contingent if it is neither necessarily true nor necessarily false.

Accidental properties are contingent (e.g., the design of this book is dependent on specific designers and could have been different), but in philosophy, the word 'contingent' is used to describe truths or events as well. For instance, it is (one might argue) entirely contingent that Grace Jones's album *Nightclubbing* was released on 11 May 1981 (it might just as well have been released on the 4th). Similarly, the statement, 'My name is Adam' is true depending on who utters it – if it's me, it's true; if it's someone called Jonathan, it's false.

Contingency is usually contrasted with necessity and appears most prominently in discussions about modality (the subfield of metaphysics that focuses on possibility). Discussions about modality are often framed in terms of 'possible worlds'. A possible world is an alternative reality (which most people think are hypothetical). They are worlds different to our own, diverging in small to much larger ways. In one (nearby) possible world, my name is Alan, not Adam. In another (much more distant) possible world, I'm called Adam, but I'm a cyborg. In an even further possible world, I'm a magical flying newt (some would deny this is in any way a possibility). Necessary truths are realized in *all* possible worlds, while contingent truths are only found in some.

In a nutshell
Something is contingent if it need not have been the case.

Why it matters
Contingency is a central conceptual strut in our understanding of what is and isn't possible.

Key figures
Ruth Barcan Marcus 1921–2012
Dorothy Edgington, b.1941
Gottlob Frege, 1848–1925

Make the connection
false, p.10
subjective, p.76
relativism, p.107

a priori

How do you know that $1 + 1 = 2$? It's not as if you need to experiment. *A priori* is a Latin phrase that means 'from what comes before'. It refers to knowledge that is independent of empirical observation. It is knowledge that can be known or justified independently of sensory experience and is derived instead through rational deliberation and the analysis of concepts.

Mathematical truths are understood to be *a priori*, as are logical truths like 'a triangle has three sides' and 'all grizzly bears are mammals'. You don't need to do a survey of all bears in order to know this. Certain metaphysical principles, like the Law of Non-Contradiction (which holds that contradictory propositions can't both be true in the same sense at the same time) are also thought to be known *a priori*. It is, understandably, the preferred form of knowledge for the rationalists, who tend to worry about the reliability of sense data.

Why do philosophers use Latin to describe this type of knowledge? Scholars in the Euro-American tradition use Latin as a rhetorical flourish. It's fancy (even more so when it's *italicized*). They also use Latin to prevent non-philosophers from understanding what they're talking about. That is, it's a way to exclude people, especially those who don't have a Classical education. If you look through this book, you'll see this isn't the first time that knowledge of Latin – or Greek – has proven useful in understanding philosophical concepts.

In a nutshell
Describes knowledge that can be gleaned without recourse to sense data.

Why it matters
For rationalists, *a priori* knowledge is immune to the confusions and corruptions of sense data and material evidence.

Key figures
Ruth Barcan Marcus, 1921–2012
René Descartes, 1596–1650
Jennifer Nagel
Linda Zagzebski, b.1946

Make the connection
knowledge, p.8
rationalism, p.69
analysis, p.84

I know.

a posteriori

A posteriori is another fancy Latin phrase and means 'from what comes after'. Unlike *a priori* knowledge, which you know *prior* to empirical investigation, *a posteriori* is gleaned *after* ('posterior to') empirical observation. It is derived from evidence provided by the external world.

For instance, it's only by turning your attention to the external world that you can learn (either directly or through indirect means, such as the internet) that in January 2024, the Bhutanese Prime Minister was Dasho Tshering Tobgay. It doesn't matter how much conceptual analysis you perform, this truth is only gleaned when you look to the world. This holds for scientific facts and experiential knowledge.

Rationalists are usually contrasted with empiricists, who privilege *a posteriori* knowledge. Their Latin dictum is *Nihil in intellectu quod prius non fuerit in sensu*, which means 'There is nothing in the mind that wasn't first in the senses.' When it comes to the seemingly *a priori* truth 1 + 1 = 2, a strict empiricist might say it depends on our observation of single things being added together (we see that one orange added to another orange makes two oranges).

Of the two types of knowledge, *a priori* is often considered to have a higher degree of certainty because it relies on reason and necessary truths rather than our, sometimes unreliable, senses. The conceptual distinction between *a priori* and *a posteriori* is used, not so much to discredit claims, but rather to analyse the foundations of knowledge.

In a nutshell
A posteriori knowledge is gleaned from sense data.

Why it matters
A posteriori knowledge constitutes the majority of scientific learning.

Key figures
A. J. Ayer, 1910–1989
Francis Bacon, 1561–1626
Nancy Cartwright, b.1944
Evelyn Fox Keller, 1936–2023

Make the connection
knowledge, p.8
deduction, p.61
empiricism, p.68

substratum

Let's think about a chair. It's a red chair and has your name written across the seat. It's a cool chair with cool designs on the back. We can write out a list of properties this chair has, some of which it has essentially (by definition) and some of which we can change: it has four legs, it's painted red, it has cool designs. You get the idea.

What, exactly, is the thing that has these properties? What is the object that has your name written on it? It's a wooden chair, so we might say it's the wood that has these properties. But the wood has properties too. It has a grain and it's flammable. It's breakable and can give you splinters. What is the thing that has *these* properties?

This train of thought has led some people to the idea of a substratum. *Substratum* is Latin for 'what lies beneath' ('stratum' is a term used in geology to describe a layer of rock; substratum is the layer that lies beneath all the other layers). Substratum is, supposedly, the underlying stuff that endures through changes in properties. It is the bearer of these properties, the thing that undergoes change.

Substratum is a helpful concept when trying to explain how objects can lose properties and gain new ones, but it's controversial. The notion of bare substrata – of property-less substance – seems almost nonsensical. It's certainly hard to keep in mind something that doesn't have any attributes and exists independently of them.

In a nutshell
The bare bearer of properties.

Why it matters
This philosophical concept has a long and surprisingly illustrious history, but is now widely rejected (along with similar peculiar concepts such as *quiddity* or *haecceity*).

Key figures
Duns Scotus, 1265–1308
John Locke, 1632–1704
A. N. Whitehead, 1861–1947
David Wiggins, b.1933

Make the connection
existence, p.70
subsistence, p.71
ontology, p.114

substance

From the Latin *sub*, meaning 'under', and *stantia*, meaning 'standing', a substance is not necessarily something we understand, but the thing that 'stands under'. It is, like substrata, that which persists through changes in properties. Unlike substrata, however, substances are not property-less.

An oak tree is an example of a substance, or a 'primary substance', as Aristotelians would call it. The oak is a specific entity, which lives in a particular kind of way. It starts life as a seed, which then germinates, grows leaves, photosynthesizes and releases oxygen. Its properties are constantly changing (it becomes bigger, grows and loses branches, sheds leaves in the winter). The matter that makes up this substance is constantly changing too: the plant cells (and the chemicals that constitute them) are being replaced all the time.

When metaphysicians talk about substances, they're not talking about property-less stuff, but about entities with a particular mode of existence. In the Aristotelian tradition, the paradigmatic substances are organisms – like trees and cats and dogs and humans – which all have a unique (and different) way of being in the world. For Cartesian 'dualists', meanwhile, there are two types of substance: mind and body.

The term 'substance' generally refers to independently existing entities with specific properties and modes of being, while 'substratum' refers to an underlying, unobservable entity that supports observable properties.

In a nutshell
A metaphysical entity (in some systems, it is considered the most fundamental type of entity).

Why it matters
According to the British metaphysician David Wiggins, our day-to-day activities rely on our idea of substances – of discrete, individual things that persist through time, while changing parts.

Key figures
Aristotle,
*c.*384–322 BCE
Sandra Harding, b.1935
David Wiggins, b.1933
Charlotte Witt

Make the connection
identity, p.6
subsistence, p.71
accidental, p.78

analysis

The word 'analysis' comes from the Greek *ana* and *luein*, which means 'loosen up'! It's a process of examination that involves disassembly. Complex ideas and problems are broken down into their constituent parts – the various claims and principles – in order to gain a deeper understanding of their nature and implications.

Philosophical analysis involves an examination of the logical structure of arguments or statements. It focuses on clarifying language by, for instance, disambiguating terms. An analysis of the term 'analysis' would need to take into account the fact that it has different meanings, which can cause confusion.

Another prominent use of the term relates to psychoanalysis, a therapeutic practice that revolves around an analyst's engagement with a subject's unconscious. People who undergo psychoanalysis are said to go 'through analysis' (they're loosened up). Were you to look at the vast psychoanalytic literature, you would find the terms 'analysis' and 'analytic' being used in significantly different ways to how they're used in analytic philosophy.

Analytic philosophy is a tradition that emphasizes clarity of language, the disassembly of problems, precision in argumentation and a rigorous unpicking of concepts. It's more similar to the scientific method than to the interpretative approach of many other disciplines in the humanities. Emerging in the early twentieth century, primarily in the Anglophone world, it remains one of the dominant approaches in contemporary philosophy.

In a nutshell
A process of examination.

Why it matters
The process of analysis offers (in principle) insights into otherwise opaque or seemingly mundane phenomena.

Key figures
Ruth Barcan Marcus, 1921–2012
G. E. Moore, 1873–1958
Bertrand Russell, 1872–1970
Ludwig Wittgenstein, 1889–1951

Make the connection
contradiction, p.64
validity, p.72
disjunction, p.117

analytic

In discussions about philosophical logic, 'analytic' can refer to a type of statement, which is true in virtue of its meaning and the definitions of the terms used. The truth of the statement (it's 'truth value') is not dependent on empirical observations (statements that *are* dependent in this way are sometimes called 'synthetic').

Consider the statement 'All grizzly bears are mammals.' The truth of this claim is inherent in the definition of the term 'bears' (a type of mammal). In this sense, analytic statements tend to be self-evident or tautological, i.e., they are true because they restate the same idea in different words.

Analytic statements also tend to be *a priori*, insofar as their truth can be determined without any need to investigate the external world. Views about this diverge. 'Water boils at 100 degrees Celsius at standard atmospheric pressure' appears to be an analytic statement, because it's based on the definitions of water, boiling and temperature. It's arguable, however, that the specific temperature at which water boils may be something we've learned through empirical observation and experimentation.

What is the point of analytic statements, if they simply restate the same idea in different terms? They don't provide new factual information, but help clarify the meanings of terms and concepts.

In a nutshell
An analytic statement is one that is true in virtue of the definition of the terms contained within it.

Why it matters
'Analyticity' (as it is called) gives us a more fine-grained way to understand arguments and logical systems.

Key figures
Sandra Harding, b.1935
Sally Haslanger, b.1955
Saul Kripke, 1940–2022
Marguerite La Caze

Make the connection

nihilism

One of the biggest obstacles to understanding nihilism is probably popular culture. In the public imagination, nihilists dress in black polo necks, wear berets and smoke cigarettes. 'God is dead,' they say, while sipping coffee, 'life is meaningless.'

Nihilists don't have special costumes. They don't even have to be particularly miserable. The term 'nihilist' can simply be used to refer to someone who denies the existence of something. A 'mereological nihilist', for instance, is someone who denies the existence of composite objects (and holds that the only existing things are microscopic, indivisible entities). 'Logical nihilists', meanwhile, believe that there is no correct, robust logical system.

Normally when we talk about nihilism we're referring to an existential nihilism that denies any inherent meaning or value in existence. If someone tells you that they're a nihilist, you can assume they're sceptical about social structures and moral values. A nihilist believes, not in God or a Greater Purpose, nor in tradition and social institutions, but in nothing (*nihil* is Latin for 'nothing').

It can sound dramatic ('I believe in *nothing*!') and there's something edgy about nihilism. On one level, it's a reactionary position – 'Whatever it is, we're against it!' – but it can be a generative approach to standard philosophical questions, encouraging a reanalysis of long-held assumptions and beliefs.

In a nutshell
The denial of the existence of various things, including God, morality and meaning.

Why it matters
It can be an important political stance as well as a metaphysical one. At one time, for instance, the denial of the existence of God would have been read as a revolutionary act.

Key figures
Albert Camus, 1913–1960
Calvin L. Warren
Cornel West, b.1953

Make the connection
existence, p.70
postmodernism, p.110
materialism, p.124

fatalism

Fatalism is the view that, regardless of our aims, hopes and ambitions, the future is already written. Our lives unfold in predetermined ways irrespective of our attempted interventions. For the fatalist, events are 'fated'. Since we can't change anything, the healthiest response is to resign ourselves to our inescapable futures.

A fatalistic attitude is, on the face of it, quite similar to a nihilistic one. Neither nihilists nor fatalists have an abundance of hope. But the routes by which they reach this hopelessness are quite different. The nihilist denies the existence of meaning. There is no Greater Purpose, no Grand Plan for humanity, there's nothing. By contrast, the fatalist believes in fate. There is an overarching trajectory to the human story – something close to, if not exactly, destiny. The problem is that this fate undermines the possibility of agency and therefore (the argument goes) the meaningfulness of our actions.

The fatalistic view may lead to resignation. More positively, it may encourage us to accept situations we would otherwise rail against. Unlike nihilism, fatalism doesn't deny the existence of meaning, but shifts the focus away from the perceived impact of human actions. Nihilism leaves room for human agency; it remains possible for the nihilist to create meaning for him- or herself, even if there's no inherent meaning in life.

In a nutshell
The view that some things (maybe all things) happen inevitably.

Why it matters
If we're too committed to fatalism, we may hold back from acting, even when action is politically important.

Key figures
Democritus,
c.460–370 BCE
Emily Dickinson,
1830–1886
Friedrich Nietzsche,
1844–1900
Arthur Schopenhauer,
1788–1860

Make the connection
pessimism, p.100
indeterminism, p.130
inescapability, p.148

consciousness

A couple of years ago, I had eye surgery. I was given a general anaesthetic and, just before the surgeon started the operation, I lost consciousness. The next thing I knew I was 'coming to' in the hospital bed, with an ache in my eye and a bandage round my head. I 'regained consciousness'. But what was it I lost and found again?

Consciousness is the state of being aware, of being able to perceive both external stimuli (the smell of the ward, the pain in my eye) and mental states (the anxiety before being 'put under', the relief on waking up). If you're conscious of something, you're aware of it. You may not be conscious during a dreamless sleep, but if you're dreaming, you're aware of *something* (even if it isn't real).

Consciousness is the state of being aware, but you can be aware of something without being conscious of it. Sometimes we talk about 'subconscious' awareness, which relates to things that happen below the conscious level. You might, for instance, have certain subconscious thoughts that shape your awareness without you really realizing (for example, you might subconsciously think your employer is attractive, which may be why you're always nervous around them). We also talk about unconscious awareness. In psychoanalysis, 'the unconscious' is an entity that perceives, acts and interacts, often in opposition to the conscious mind.

I'm aware!

self-consciousness

Most of the time if you describe someone as 'self-conscious', you probably think they're 'uncomfortable in their own skin'. They're awkward: overly aware of what they're doing, what they're saying, how they're standing, and so on. But self-consciousness has a broader meaning. It refers to a specific aspect of consciousness, which involves being aware of oneself. Self-consciousness goes beyond mere awareness of external stimuli and includes the ability to reflect on one's own mental states and recognize oneself as a subject of experience.

A lot of animals are conscious creatures. They feel pain, affection and terror. They can see, taste, touch and smell. There are also quite a few who don't seem to be conscious at all (like molluscs). Only a handful are self-conscious, and humans, I think, are among them. Cognitively speaking, we can do all of the things a conscious creature does, but we can also actually think of ourselves undergoing these conscious experiences. We can recognize ourselves as individuals, who ruminate and find jokes funny and reflect on our everyday understanding of consciousness.

Because self-consciousness allows us to examine our*selves*, it is often associated with higher-level cognitive development and the awareness of oneself as an individual. While consciousness involves the ability to introspect – to look inside yourself and be aware of your mental states – self-consciousness specifically involves introspection about your mental states as *your* mental states.

In a nutshell
The capacity to consider yourself as yourself.

Why it matters
It is a mark of higher cognitive ability, which many have argued forms the foundation for freedom and moral responsibility.

Key figures
Patricia Churchland, b.1943
Donna Haraway, b.1944
Martin Heidegger, 1889–1976
Susan Wolf, b.1952

Make the connection
identity, p.6
phenomenology, p.118
epiphenomenalism, p.153

identity politics

How you or I, or anyone else, experiences society depends on where we stand in it. People who are well-off, for example, experience it differently from those who are struggling to make ends meet. The same is true for women and men in sexist societies, just as it is for racially minoritized people and white folk in white supremacist societies. Your social position affects what experiences you're exposed to.

This doesn't mean it's impossible for a person to understand how members of other social groups experience society, but understanding is not the same as feeling. I can understand the effect of the long histories of a racist police force, but as a white person I can't have 'lived' or 'first-hand' experience of anti-Black policing.

Thoughts such as these move us to think that an individual's identity characteristics are politically significant. Identity characteristics (i.e., characteristics that allow us to identify individuals, and that allow individuals to understand themselves) include race, gender, sexual orientation, ethnicity and religion.

'Identity politics' refers to political and social movements that focus on the concerns and interests of specific groups, based on these sorts of shared traits. It emphasizes how individuals within these groups face specific challenges and are subject to particular experiences.

In a nutshell
An approach to political discussions that foregrounds identity characteristics such as race, gender and sexual orientation.

Why it matters
Arguing for or against the importance of identity is one of the political fault-lines in mainstream discourse.

Key figures
Gloria Anzaldúa, 1942–2004
Pierre Bourdieu, 1930–2002
Audre Lorde, 1934–1992

Make the connection
identity, p.6
empathy, p.26
double consciousness, p.136

intersectionality

Some people worry that identity politics reduces individuals to identity characteristics, oversimplifying issues by understanding them in relation to, for instance, race or gender, in a way that can be divisive. In some sense, intersectionality responds to this concern. The term was brought into mainstream usage by civil-rights advocate Kimberlé Crenshaw in the late 1980s. Essentially, an intersectional approach is one that recognizes that individuals hold multiple social identities, which intersect and interact.

An intersectional analysis of a white working-class man, for example, would consider race, class and gender. Being white in a racist society, he would experience certain privileges and expectations. Being a man in a sexist society, he would have gender privileges and expectations, too (e.g., to conform to traditional notions of masculinity). Being working-class, he would face economic challenges and limited access to resources. The combination of these identities creates distinctive social expectations.

Different identities intersect, leading to a unique experience of the social world. When you mix identities, you don't just get a collection of identities, you get something new, just as, when you mix eggs, flour and sugar, you get a cake, and not just a messy collection of ingredients.

While identity politics focuses on political mobilization around specific identity categories, intersectionality is a framework for understanding the complexities of multiple identities and encourages a more holistic approach to social analysis.

In a nutshell
An examination of how, for any individual, different roles, identities and social expectations interact.

Why it matters
Intersectionality is one of the most nuanced ways to frame and understand someone's social position.

Key figures
Patricia Hill Collins, b.1948
Shirley Anne Tate, b.1956
Isabel Wilkerson, b.1961
Mary Wollstonecraft, 1759–1797

Make the connection
equity, p.19
prejudice, p.50

communism

'Workers of the world, unite! You have nothing to lose but your chains!' So wrote Karl Marx and Friedrich Engels in their *Communist Manifesto* of 1848. It's a catchy slogan, but what exactly does it mean? The aim of communism is the establishment of a classless and stateless society. A stateless society is one without a government, i.e., there's no state, just a community of equals.

Within this community of equals, goods (like food) and services (like healthcare) would be distributed according to individual needs. Another guiding communist maxim (from Marx's *Critique of the Gotha Programme*) is 'from each according to their ability, to each according to their need'. Within communism, individuals contribute to society based on their abilities and everyone receives support according to their requirements. If, for instance, you're elderly and infirm, you wouldn't be expected to do heavy manual labour and you would receive hospital treatment when it was necessary.

Another central communist ambition is collective ownership of the means of production – that is, the estates and tools required to make products and provide resources. In other social configurations, including capitalist ones, factories and workspaces are owned by private individuals or companies, who employ labourers. The labourers (the 'working class') are reliant on their employers in order to ply their trade (e.g., printers need printing presses). Collective ownership would empower labourers and, so the argument goes, release them from the exploitative chains of capitalism.

In a nutshell
A political ideology that aims at establishing a stateless and classless society.

Why it matters
Attempts at communism, and resistance to them, have shaped the political landscape for over a century.

Key figures
Friedrich Engels, 1820–1895
Rosa Luxembourg, 1871–1919
Karl Marx, 1818–1883

Make the connection
liberalism, p.47
hegemony, p.67
capitalism, p.98

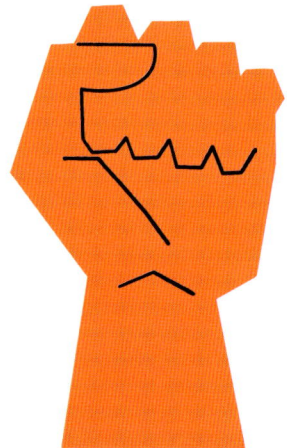

socialism

Like communism, socialism advocates shared ownership of property and the means of production. Socialists, however, argue for stronger state involvement. Public ownership, they argue, should be organized and regulated by a government; public transport is a good example of a state-led service. That is to say, socialists tend to think there should be a political body that oversees the community of equals, made up of members of that community.

A socialist government would also be expected to intervene in order to ensure the welfare of citizens and to address economic inequalities between them. This would involve the equal distribution of goods, in the form of a universal basic income, for example, or a National Health Service.

Socialism doesn't always require the complete abolition of private property (there are different forms of socialism, just as there are different forms of communism and capitalism), but socialists recognize that private property ownership can lead to inequalities.

Rather than providing an alternative to communism, socialism is often understood to be a stepping stone from capitalism – where property is privately owned for private benefit – to a society where everything is communally owned and used for the community's benefit (communism). Countries like Sweden, Norway and Denmark are often cited as examples of democracies guided by strong socialist principles such as free education, universal social insurance and progressive taxation (where higher-income individuals are taxed at higher rates).

In a nutshell
A political ideology that advocates shared, public ownership, but isn't committed to the dissolution of the state.

Why it matters
Socialist principles inform many governments around the world.

Key figures
C. L. R. James
1901–1989
Martin Luther King, Jr., 1929–1968
Helen Keller, 1880–1968
Bertrand Russell, 1872–1970

Make the connection
ideology, p.66
neoliberalism, p.99

is

One of the shortest words in the English language is also one of the trickiest. Very *very* roughly, we might say 'is' indicates a state of existence or identity. It's a form of the verb 'to be'. In English, it also links the subject of a sentence (what the sentence is about) to a predicate (which describes what the subject is doing). For example, 'The cat [the subject] is sleeping [the predicate]' or 'This book [the subject] is confusing [the predicate]'.

'Is' and the verb 'to be' feature prominently in metaphysics, the area of philosophy that examines questions of existence. To say that something *is* is to say that it *exists*. Subject–predicate statements like 'The cat is sleeping' also make claims about reality. It really, truly is the case that the cat is sleeping. If we weren't so sure about this, we might say 'The cat *appears* to be sleeping' or 'The cat *seems* to be sleeping.'

In a naive understanding of metaphysics, claims about the state of reality are value-free. They're supposed to be objective, outside the realm of opinion or taste. Whether or not the cat is sleeping isn't a matter of perspective, it's a fact. But metaphysics is a human practice, as susceptible as any other to bias, prejudice and conceptual confusions. We see this in the ease with which some people slip between claims about what *is* and claims about what *ought* to be ...

In a nutshell
'Is' indicates a state of existence and links subjects to predicates.

Why it matters
It allows us to make claims about reality.

Key figures
Aristotle, 384–323 BCE
Alexius Meinong, 1853–1920
W. V. O. Quine, 1908–2000
Alfred Tarski, 1901–1983

Make the connection
objective, p.77
existence, p.70
ontology, p.114

ought

'Ought' is an odd word. It seems incomplete, a half-finished thought. On the whole it has dropped from common usage, largely replaced by the less formal 'should'. Both 'ought' and 'should' are used in statements that express moral or ethical judgements. Unlike 'is' statements, 'ought' statements don't describe reality, but convey a sense of obligation or duty. 'You ought to apologize', for instance, or 'You should never speak ill of the dead'. The focus is on value judgements, moral principles and normative considerations. 'Normative', here, relates to what counts as 'normal', e.g., what kind of cutlery one usually uses to consume soup (spoons and not straws).

Many philosophical and religious traditions see a strong connection between how the world is and how we *ought* to behave. Homophobia, a mainstay of various religious traditions, is often expressed in relation to nature. 'Homosexuality just isn't natural,' people say. There is a (mistaken) belief that homosexuality doesn't occur in nature. This supposed fact is taken to support the claim that we shouldn't be gay. 'Is' is taken to imply 'ought'. Homosexuality is unnatural, the argument goes, therefore we shouldn't be homosexual. It's an example of what's known as the naturalistic fallacy – the (mistaken) belief that just because something is natural it is necessarily right.

In a nutshell
When you describe what ought to be, you're saying what you think should be the case.

Why it matters
It's how people express and enforce moral opinions.

Key figures
Carol J. Adams, b.1951
David Hume, 1711–1776
Immanuel Kant, 1724–1804
Christine Korsgaard, b.1952

Make the connection
biological, p.24
morality, p.38
normal, p.134

I ought to be better.

OUGHT

scientific

These days academic philosophy is considered to be a humanities subject, falling alongside literature, art, history and theology rather than physics, chemistry or the other sciences. Part of the reason for this is the way philosophy is practised. Most of the time, you can pursue 'armchair' theorizing – reading books, hypothesizing, testing your intuitions and examining the consistency of your arguments. That is, there's no need to actually gather empirical data, to conduct surveys or to prioritize evidence-based reasoning, which are all approaches associated with the 'scientific method'.

Science aims to understand, explain and predict natural phenomena through systematic inquiries and a combination of inferential, inductive and deductive reasoning (see pages 11, 60–61). A scientific inquiry into taste, for instance, may involve chemical analyses of strong flavours or a microscopic observation of tastebuds. A philosophical inquiry into taste, by contrast, might involve a discussion of beauty, an analysis of sweetness and an exploration of aesthetic objectivity – none of which would necessarily require you to find your way to a laboratory.

However some philosophers put a premium on the scientific method. They argue that philosophy would do well to rely more heavily on empirical investigation. The Logical Positivists, who flourished in the early twentieth century and heavily influenced the Analytic movement, thought we should stop debating speculative claims that can't be empirically tested or verified, e.g., how many angels can dance on the head of a pin? Why (the Logical Positivists ask) should we care?

In a nutshell
The scientific method refers to a set of principles and evidence-based procedures used to explain reality.

Why it matters
This method is one of the main ways that humans generate knowledge about the world.

Key figures
Valerie Gray Hardcastle
Sandra Harding, b.1935
Susan Oyama, b.1943
Kim Sterelny, b.1950

Make the connection
inference, p.11
induction, p.60
analysis, p.84
realism, p.106

scientistic

While some think philosophy should be modelled on the sciences, emphasizing evidence-based reasoning, others resist what they see as a 'scientistic' attitude. 'Scientistic' refers to an exaggerated or unwarranted belief in the authority and scope of scientific methods and knowledge. If you call an approach 'scientistic', you're suggesting that it's making a fetish of science, applying the scientific method to everything, indiscriminately.

Imagine, for instance, that you want to investigate the particular kind of yearning nostalgia that you experience when you return to your childhood home. You might think, as I do, that an analysis of your hormone levels and a map of the neurons firing in your brain would provide only a partial picture of that multifaceted experience. The angst, the longing, the memories of an irretrievable youth arguably cannot be explored exclusively through observation and the collection of falsifiable data sets. To understand this kind of complex experience, you need to engage with abstract, historical and sometimes metaphorical claims, drawing on poetry, literature and the arts, as well as philosophical debates about the nature of love, and time, and homesickness.

In short, being scientific involves the disciplined pursuit of knowledge through empirical means, while 'scientistic' describes an over-reliance on (or misapplication of) scientific principles and methods, often at the cost of more nuanced understandings of the world.

In a nutshell
Scientism is the excessive belief in the power of the scientific method.

Why it matters
By focusing on scientific achievements, we can lose sight of the insights offered by other knowledge systems.

Key figures
Evelyn Fox Keller, 1936–2023
Donna Haraway, b.1944
Mary Midgley, 1919–2018
Arianne Shahvisi

Make the connection
ideology, p.66
subjective, p.76
postmodernism, p.110

capitalism

Capitalism is an economic system characterized by private ownership of the means of production. It is market driven, which is to say that prices depend on the demand (in the market) for products and the ease with which they can be supplied. 'Capital' refers to both financial capital (i.e., the money used to start businesses) and physical capital (the means of production).

How does all of that work in practice? Well, this afternoon – horror of horrors! – I ran out of apples. I went to the supermarket and bought a bag of five, which set me back £2.50, and now I'm thinking I should invest in an apple tree. Except that I'd need a garden to grow it, and even then it would only produce apples at certain times of the year. The supermarket buys its apples from suppliers who have orchards across the globe, which is why they can provide apples all year round. The suppliers are a private company, who own the orchards and employ labourers at little over minimum wage, to pick, package and ship the produce. The company has been able to expand because its business model creates a profit. It's a capitalist business; the means of production (the orchards and packaging facilities) are owned by a private company (the suppliers) that employs labourers (who *don't* own any part of the business) to make money. The supermarket is also a capitalist business.

In a nutshell
A pervasive political, ideological and economic system, characterized by private ownership of the means of production.

Why it matters
It is one of the dominant ideologies in the modern world.

Key figures
Milton Friedman, 1912–2006
Karl Marx, 1818–1883
John Maynard Keynes, 1883–1946
Adam Smith, 1723–1790

Make the connection
ideology, p.66
communism, p.92

neoliberalism

Neoliberalism is the economic form of liberalism, an ideology that holds citizens should be free to do as they please, as long as it doesn't negatively impact (harm) others. Neoliberals emphasize 'free-market' capitalism. That is, they advocate for reducing barriers to trade, such as high taxation and other forms of government intervention. They think the market should be free to develop according to customers' needs and desires.

Neoliberals also encourage private ownership of the means of production. The rationale here is that a competitive marketplace – where private companies are competing against each other to meet customer demand – will be better for consumers. Competition, the argument goes, can lead to the lowering of prices, greater innovation and improved products. The privatization of public services, like national rail companies or healthcare provisions, is a neoliberal phenomenon, underwritten by the belief that profit-driven competition between privately owned companies will lead to better customer experiences, as each company vies for more customers.

Capitalism is a general economic system characterized by private ownership of capital and a focus on creating profit. Neoliberalism, on the other hand, is more specific, advocating for economic and political policies (e.g., lower taxation) within a capitalist framework. Neoliberalism is a particular policy orientation within the broader context of capitalism.

In a nutshell
Neoliberalism holds that citizens should be free to conduct business as they please (as long as it doesn't harm others).

Why it matters
Neoliberal policies are among the most popular economic policies in nation–states around the world.

Key figures
John Rawls, 1921–2002
Ronald Reagan, 1911–2004
Tommie Shelby
Margaret Thatcher, 1925–2013

Make the connection
power, p.41
liberalism, p.47
socialism, p.93

pessimism

People are always telling me not to be so pessimistic. What they mean by this, I think, is that I should be more upbeat about the future. I shouldn't always expect the worst. 'Cheer up,' they say, 'it might never happen!' Unfortunately, it almost always does.

Pessimism, usually understood to be the opposite of optimism, is a general tendency to see the negative and to anticipate unfavourable outcomes. It is an attitude that affects your perception of events ('That disaster was bound to happen'), though it doesn't necessarily imply you think badly of people, or believe that they can't have good intentions. Pessimists tend to think that good people with good intentions are fine, as it goes, but that they will rarely if ever succeed in their projects. For instance, I might be pessimistic about the outcome of this writing work. I genuinely want to produce a book that is readable, informative and critically engaged, but despite the fact that I'm trying quite hard, I'm not confident I'll be able to achieve the desired result.

You might think there are advantages to a pessimistic outlook. If you expect the worst, you'll be pleasantly surprised when something good happens. Unfortunately, pessimism can be a disposition that colours past events as much as expectations for the future. If you're a pessimist, whatever happens or happened, you'll likely think that nothing good can come of it.

In a nutshell
A belief that the worst will almost certainly happen.

Why it matters
Whether or not you are pessimistic will affect your ambitions and approach to challenges.

Key figures
Ta-Nehisi Coates, b.1975
Friedrich Nietzsche, 1844–1900
Arthur Schopenhauer, 1788–1860
Cornel West, b.1953

Make the connection
fatalism, p.87
inescapability, p.148

cynicism

Where pessimism is all-encompassing in its outlook, cynicism is more targeted. Rather than having a generally downbeat attitude, the cynic is typically suspicious of others. A cynic might believe, for instance, that people are on the whole self-interested, that their motives are rarely altruistic, and that individuals primarily act out of selfishness rather than genuine concern.

If you gave a cynic a gift, they would say, 'What do you want?' The idea that someone would do something without an agenda is alien to the cynical mindset, in which a gift is given in order to enter into a system of exchange (if you give a gift, you might expect one in return).

Cynicism is conceptually quite close to scepticism, that doubtful attitude that can be part of a philosophical method, though cynicism is more focused on interpersonal relationships. Historically, the term has been used in different ways, and in its earliest incarnations in Ancient Greece it referred to a philosophical movement that challenged social expectations, rejected the pursuit of wealth and material positions (like the ascetics) and emphasized individual freedom. (The word 'cynic' comes from the Greek *kynikos*, meaning 'dog-like', possibly referring to the Cynics' unpretentious and simple lifestyle.) Those early Cynics were suspicious of the trappings of social success, and eventually 'cynical' came to refer to this suspicious attitude rather than the positive approach to radical freedom.

In a nutshell
A tendency to believe that people are primarily motivated by self-interest.

Why it matters
Depending on how cynical you are, you will be more or less likely to trust others.

Key figures
Crates of Thebes, c.365–285 BCE
Diogenes of Sinope, c.412–323 BCE
Hipparchia, c.350–280 BCE

Make the connection
scepticism, p.56
nihilism, p.86
ascetic, p.121

autocracy

In this intense form of government, political power is concentrated in the hands of a single individual, the autocrat. The autocrat is a leader – a monarch, an emperor or a dictator – with unchecked authority. They hold absolute power, free of the checks and balances of democratic institutions. They make the laws and can eliminate legal routes by which they might be deposed. They can, as a matter of course, grant political power to whomever they want. After they've had enough of running a state, they can stipulate future leaders (e.g., their children).

Autocratic rule is often characterized by crackdowns on dissent, as well as a lack of political pluralism. Political pluralism is an approach to governance that supports the existence of diverse and sometimes competing political groups and ideologies. Within an autocracy, there may be little room for a democratic party or a party that advocates republicanism (i.e., a system where the head of state is an elected or appointed official).

However autocracies are not always so obviously repressive. It is conceptually possible, within autocracies, for institutions to have power. And while autocracies involve a concentration of political power, this form of governance doesn't necessarily entail extensive state intervention into every aspect of society. Some autocrats are content to let people get on with their day-to-day lives (just as long as they don't revolt).

In a nutshell
A political system in which power ultimately rests in the hands of a single individual.

Why it matters
Most people think autocracies are unjust political systems and need to be resisted.

Key figures
Hannah Arendt, 1906–1975
Michel Foucault, 1926–1984
Thomas Hobbes, 1588–1679
Jean-Jacques Rousseau, 1712–1778

Make the connection
domination, p.53
hegemony, p.67
capitalism, p.98

totalitarianism

Totalitarianism is another intense form of governance, in which the state tries (and sometimes succeeds) to control every aspect of public and private life. Totalitarianism involves the government's *total* control of the population; state intervention is, therefore, extensive and commonplace. This can mean greater surveillance (security cameras on every street corner, regular checks on domestic arrangements) and pervasive propaganda intended to shape the attitudes of the citizenry (totalitarianism often involves state ownership of media outlets).

While autocrats can, perhaps, give their citizens some (restricted) freedoms, a totalitarian state government is necessarily much more involved in the social sphere and everyday lives of the population. It is a hostile environment for political pluralism, since such pluralism would challenge the single narrative of the state, i.e., that the state is all-powerful, all-good and always right. The totalitarian state controls political mechanisms, but also social and cultural products. Books that provide or celebrate alternative ways of living, for example, would be destroyed.

An autocracy can be totalitarian if the autocrat seeks to be in total control, but this isn't inevitable. Likewise, a totalitarian state may be ruled by an autocrat, but it might equally be ruled by a group of elected officials (whose control over the population may be so powerful that they can ensure their own repeated re-election).

In a nutshell
Involves the state's total control over the citizenry.

Why it matters
It is a repressive and dangerous form of governance.

Key figures
Hannah Arendt, 1906–1975
Isaiah Berlin, 1909–1997
Niccolò Machiavelli, 1469–1527
Iris Marion Young, 1040–2006

Make the connection
liberalism, p.47
oppression, p.52
socialism, p.93

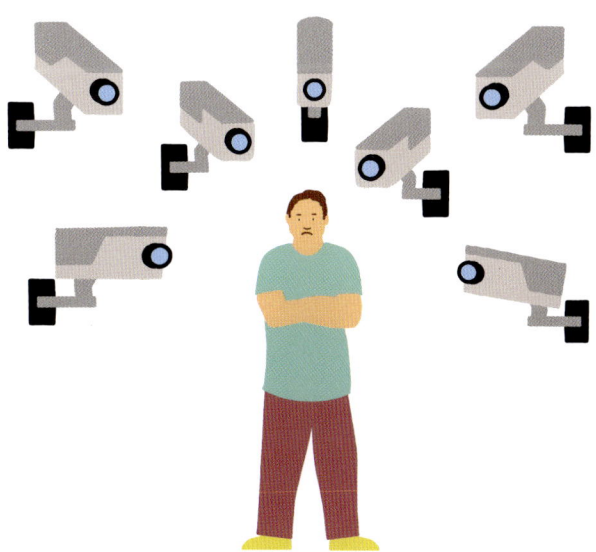

synthetic

Polyester, it turns out, makes me terribly itchy. This might be because it's what's known as a 'synthetic' fabric. Unlike cotton, which comes from a plant, or wool, which comes from woolly mammals, synthetic fabrics are chemically produced, from petroleum, using a process called polymerization. Here, 'synthetic' refers to something fabricated, rather than something naturally occurring.

Usually, when we describe something as synthetic, we mean that it's made by humans. More precisely, synthetic suggests that the object is *synthesized* (the clue's in the name), i.e., that it's made through the (often chemical) synthesis, or bringing together, of components or elements.

The term 'synthetic' is used in formal logic to describe statements that are distinct from 'analytic' statements. While the truth of an analytic statement is determined through analysis of the terms being used (e.g., 'All pentagons have five sides'), synthetic statements require empirical evidence in order to be verified. 'The cat is on the mat' is true only if the cat is actually on the mat. Another technical use of the term 'synthetic', or 'synthesis' – closer to our everyday usage – relates to a particular kind of argumentative structure. One could offer a 'thesis' (a provisional claim or argument), which might be met by an 'antithesis' (an opposing claim or argument). A 'synthesis' is a combination of the two positions – a middle ground that allows the argument to move forward.

In a nutshell
'Synthetic' can refer to a type of logical statement as well as human-made materials.

Why it matters
It's an everyday word with multiple (confusing) meanings.

Key figures
Donna Haraway, b.1944
Georg Wilhelm Friedrich Hegel, 1770–1831
Gillian Russell

Make the connection
natural, p.25
scientific, p.96
posthumanism, p.133

artificial

The terms 'synthetic' and 'artificial' are often used interchangeably (although not in formal logic or in describing an argumentative structure). In everyday language, both refer to something that's made or produced by humans, rather than being natural. However, there are important, if subtle, differences.

An artificial object is one made by human skill, or 'art', perhaps through the efforts of an 'artisan'. The word 'artificial' doesn't necessarily indicate the fabrication process – artificial objects aren't necessarily created through chemical synthesis, for example – but it implies that the object may in some way be an *imitation* of something else. Artificial flavourings like sweeteners are supposed to replicate the taste of so-called 'natural' flavours like sugar. Artificial intelligence is supposed to match or mirror human intelligence. Our everyday use of these terms suggests that artificial objects have some counterpart in nature, while synthetic ones do not.

Nevertheless, both types of objects are human-made, and, according to some metaphysical traditions (which examine *how* things exist), they are in a certain sense less real than natural objects. Human-made things, like plastic flowers, do not hang together in the same way as real flowers. Pretty though they may be, they are also considerably less complex: they don't grow, they don't rot, they are not living.

In a nutshell
Artificial things are created by humans to replace or imitate 'natural' objects.

Why it matters
Metaphysicians claim there is a significant distinction between naturally occurring entities and artificial ones.

Key figures
Peter van Inwagen, b.1942
Lynne Rudder Baker, 1944–2017
Michael Thompson
David Wiggins, b.1933

Make the connection
biological, p.24
substance, p.83
scientific, p.96

realism

Most people would probably say murder is objectively wrong. It's just *bad*, isn't it? It doesn't matter who you are, or where you live, or what exactly your reasons may be for doing the murder (they may even be good-ish reasons), it's just a fact: murder is wrong.

In philosophy, the term 'realism' refers to the belief that something (e.g., the external world) is real. Moral realism posits that moral principles are real; they exist, independent of society and human thought. This is what is implied when we say that an act, like murder, is *objectively* wrong. The principle of the sanctity of life, which holds that all life is sacred, and therefore that murder is a violation, is universally true and applies regardless of personal opinions or cultural norms.

In this context, realism is a 'meta-ethical' position. Meta-ethics isn't primarily focused on the question of whether this or that action is 'right' or 'virtuous'. The meta-ethicist is interested in the metaphysics of morality – in whether our judgements are derived from the external world. For the moral realist, moral truths are not decided or invented, but discovered through the application of reason. Consequently, a moral realist might argue that certain actions are right or wrong, irrespective of whether a society recognizes them as such.

In a nutshell
Moral realism is the view that there are moral facts.

Why it matters
If there are moral facts, there *should* be fewer disagreements about moral decisions.

Key figures
Christine Korsgaard, b.1952
J. L. Mackie, 1917–1981
G. E. Moore, 1873–1958

Make the connection
morality, p.38
subjective, p.76
is, p.94

relativism

'It's all relative!' In contrast to the realist, the moral relativist thinks moral principles are connected to cultural or individual perspectives (or both). The claim that murder is wrong may hold in most situations, sure, but there are certain circumstances where there's flexibility, e.g., in the midst of battle.

For the moral relativist, there is no overarching, objective moral system. There is no single 'right' way of doing things. Cultural relativists hold that moral principles are relative to a cultural context. For instance, in some cultures, polygamy, the practice of having multiple spouses simultaneously, is seen to be morally acceptable. In other cultures, it isn't. Individual relativists hold that moral judgements vary from person to person. I may believe that meat-eating is immoral, since it violates the sanctity of life; you may think it's absolutely fine, because only human lives are really sacred.

There are difficulties for both moral realism and moral relativism. For instance, realism demands a degree of confidence that may be unlicensed. Think of all the moral beliefs, once upon a time claimed to be universally true, which have turned out to be heavily context dependent (that homosexuality is immoral, for example). On the other hand, relativism may undermine the possibility of moral critique; if all moral judgements are relative, there is no firm ground to say that, for instance, homophobia is immoral.

In a nutshell
For the moral relativist, moral systems are connected to cultures.

Why it matters
If we disagree with someone's moral judgement, it helps to look at the moral system within which they're working.

Key figures
Ruth Benedict, 1887–1948
Jean–François Lyotard, 1924–1998
Mary Midgley, 1919–2018
Uma Narayan

Make the connection
ethics, p.39
descriptive, p.75

know-how

Know-how is practical knowledge – the skill and expertise acquired through experience, practice and training. I was nineteen when I learned to ride a bike. Of course, I already understood the principles (you push the pedals, which turn the wheels, and steer with the handlebars), but until my friend Stephen put me on a bicycle and helped me balance, I didn't have any real experience of pedalling. I certainly didn't have the 'know-how'.

At first I found it tricky to co-ordinate my body – to hold the handlebars level while also pushing the pedals with my feet *and* balancing. But the more I tried, the more I learned which way to twist my body, how firmly I needed to pull the brakes and, eventually, where my weight should be placed when turning.

Know-how need not always be, but quite often is, embodied knowledge. It is a matter of learning about your body, your reactions and how you physically interact with the world. Playing a musical instrument is an example, as is carpentry, and throwing a basketball into a hoop. There is a gap between understanding what you need to do and actually being able to do it. Sometimes this gap can be deeply frustrating: you know what you *want* to do but you're insufficiently dextrous, for example, to be able to achieve it.

In a nutshell
Practical knowledge acquired through experience and practice.

Why it matters
Not everything can be learned from books.

Key figures
Patricia Hill Collins, b.1948
Nancy Hartsock, 1943–2015
Ludwig Wittgenstein, 1889–1951

Make the connection
knowledge, p.8
rational, p.14
phenomenology, p.118

know-that

The understanding, which often comes prior to know-how, is know-that. I know that I need to throw the basketball in order to get it through the hoop. I know that I need to push the pedals in order to propel the bike. 'Know-that' refers to what is sometimes called 'propositional knowledge' – knowledge of propositions or '*that* statements', such as 'I know *that* the world is roughly spheroid'. Know-that involves an understanding of certain truths or information that can be expressed in sentences. I know that in order to play a heart-rending flute solo, for example, it is first necessary for me to blow into the flute.

While know-how is typically embodied, know-that is usually associated with theoretical knowledge, which, so the thought goes, isn't necessarily dependent on someone's ability to act, perform or behave in certain ways. You don't have to be able to *do* something in order to know that it's the case.

The distinction between know-how and know-that is an important one in epistemology, the branch of philosophy that examines the nature of knowledge. Among other things, it suggests that knowledge isn't all about book-learning. Despite a historical tendency, especially within academia, to privilege knowledge-that over knowledge-how, embodied skills and expertise can be knowledge just as much as theoretical understanding. Far too frequently, knowledge-how is side-lined, to the detriment of certain groups (e.g., those people excluded from the education system).

In a nutshell
Propositional knowledge, typically acquired through 'book-learning'.

Why it matters
This is one of the different types of knowledge that inform our understanding of the world.

Key figures
Kristie Dotson, b.1975
Miranda Fricker, b.1966
Dorothy E. Smith, 1926–2022
Linda Zagzebski, b.1946

Make the connection
belief, p.9
objective, p.77
analysis, p.84

postmodernism

Postmodernism draws out and critiques literary conventions as well as social norms and expectations. It's a cultural and theoretical response to the movement known as 'modernism', which reached its peak in Europe in the first half of the twentieth century and is a celebration of all things 'modern' – a rejection of tradition. Modernists embraced innovation. They experimented with form in art, literature and music, in a bid to create work that reflected the often fragmentary nature of modern life.

Modernism is characterized by an optimistic belief in the power of reason, of science and of the individual, rather than the staid social norms of the group. The modernists, who saw the world moving ever onwards, powered by industry, bought into grand narratives about political progress and Truth with a capital 'T'.

Postmodernism is a rejection of these foundational assumptions. Postmodernists are sceptical of universal, capital-T Truths, grand narratives and any suggestion of objective reality. They question the idea of discrete, coherent individuals, whether in political discourse (the 'rational citizen') or in literature (the authorial 'I'). Where modernist literature focuses on the inner life of an individual, postmodernist literature rejects the very notion of an individual and breaks literary boundaries by addressing the reader directly (as I have, occasionally, done with you). Where modernism holds that Truth is universal and objective, postmodernism sees truth as a subjective, context-dependent attitude.

In a nutshell
An intellectual movement that challenges literary conventions and emphasizes the relativity of truth.

Why it matters
Postmodernism has had a profound impact on philosophy, literature and cultural studies.

Key figures
Jean Baudrillard, 1929–2007
Donna Haraway, b.1944
Julia Kristeva, b.1941
Trinh T. Minh–ha, b.1952

Make the connection
hermeneutics, p.123
posthumanism, p.133
rhetoric, p.150

I reject the idea of a universal truth.

poststructuralism

According to structuralists like Ferdinand de Saussure, cultural, social and philosophical phenomena are best understood through an analysis of underlying structures. Literature, for instance, can be discussed in relation to the underlying structures of texts, literary forms and conventions, such as 'the hero's journey'. Common to all epic stories (the thought goes) is a hero who overcomes a series of clearly defined obstacles in order to achieve a desirable resolution. There is a structure, a blueprint, a schema that can be picked out and analysed.

While structuralists look for regularities and consistency, poststructuralists argue that our intellectual, cultural and social lives are too messy to be organized into neat grids and labelled. Literature, they say, contains contradictions and hierarchies. Stories are written in a language that is inherently unstable, and meaning is constantly fluctuating. Notions such as 'the hero's journey' are unhelpfully restrictive, necessarily overlooking the nuances of epic storytelling (and all storytelling, for that matter).

Poststructuralism is a specific theoretical movement within the broader umbrella of postmodernist thought. It is allied with 'deconstruction', or the breaking down of seemingly fixed distinctions, such as cultural and intellectual binaries. Drawing a sharp line between postmodernism and poststructuralism, then, is very much against the spirit of the two traditions, which are constantly bleeding into one another.

In a nutshell
Poststructuralism critiques the structuralists' attempts to neatly categorize phenomena.

Why it matters
It speaks to the messiness of our experiences of the world.

Key figures
Hélène Cixous, b.1937
Jacques Derrida, 1930–2004
Sylvia Wynter, b.1928

Make the connection
ideology, p.66
semantics, p.122
dialectics, p.151

I reject the idea of neat structures.

animism

Like 'animal' and 'animation', the word 'animism' comes from the Latin *anima*, sometimes translated as 'breath' and sometimes as 'soul'. These words invoke an almost intangible, even invisible force that moves objects, while moving through them. Animals are entities possessed of this force. They are en-souled (animated), as are the otherwise static pictures in an animation.

Animism is a belief system that attributes consciousness, agency and sometimes souls to entities in the natural world – even seemingly inanimate objects like rocks. It's found in various cultures around the world, from the Shinto religion in Japan to the totemism of Native Americans and the Vedic traditions of Hinduism. The Igbo people, an ethnic group in Nigeria, have a cultural system that includes animist elements. Rivers, trees, rocks and animals are believed to house spiritual forces, which are often regarded as intermediaries between the people and the supreme deity referred to as 'Chukwu' or 'Chineke'.

Animistic practices typically involve a celebration of the natural world. In Britain, nature (or 'Mother Nature') is venerated in paganism and folklore, and by the Morrismen when they perform their seasonal Morris dancing. Beliefs and superstitions about the weather, about crops and animals, are in some sense all animistic.

In a nutshell
The view that agential forces move through objects other than humans.

Why it matters
A belief system with a long history, which surfaces in our day-to-day engagement with the world.

Key figures
Maria Puig de la Bellacasa, b.1972
Linda Hogan, b.1947
Glenys Livingston, b.1954
Emma Tomalin

Make the connection
belief, p.9
natural, p.25
substance, p.83

animalism

While animists think there are spiritual forces moving throughout the natural world, animalists would probably reject the idea of such intangible forces. An animalist is someone who believes that, fundamentally, we aren't minds or souls, we're just human animals.

Animalism is a philosophical position taken within the 'personal identity debate' (see p.7). Animalists are interested in why and how we persist, and in what allows us to survive from one moment to the next despite undergoing changes (for instance, the growth of my beard and the thinning of my hair). Some people think our survival rests on continued consciousness; you're the same person as the child you once were because there is some kind of psychological continuity (evidenced, for instance, by your memories). Animalists claim that personal identity is underwritten by the continued existence of the human animal, the biological organism. If I lost all my memories or fell into a vegetative state, the animalist would say that I survived just as long as the organism did.

'Animism' refers to a belief system that attributes consciousness to various elements of the natural world. 'Animalism' is a philosophical position in which our continued survival is seen to be bound up with the continued survival of the human animals that we are. The two terms are deceptively similar, but operate in different domains and address distinct questions about the nature of existence and identity.

In a nutshell
The view that we are essentially human animals.

Why it matters
An animalist may argue that someone who is brain-dead is still in some sense alive, where a neo-Lockean would say they have ceased to exist.

Key figures
Eric Olson
Paul Snowdon,
1946–2022
David Wiggins, b.1933

Make the connection
biological, p.24
substance, p.83
consciousness, p.88

ontology

Do unicorns exist? What about numbers? I'm fairly sure that humans exist, but what about ghosts and souls? Ontology, roughly speaking, is the study of *what there is* – what sorts of stuff populate the world. Ontology forms one of the central strands of metaphysics, the area of philosophy that's focused on the study of reality.

For some, metaphysical inquiry is a matter of conducting ontological checks. You start with a long list of items, including abstract entities, organisms and paradoxical things like round-squares, and you go down it, ticking and crossing out beings depending on your understanding of existence. Do chocolate bars exist? Tick. Do holes exist? Cross?

Often, metaphysicians will appeal to the principle of parsimony when going through their ontological call sheet. They will opt for theories that require fewer entities, rather than ones that admit beings by the bucket-load. A classical atomist, for instance, will say that only atoms really, truly exist. Everything else is just bunches of atoms arranged in certain ways.

Not all ontologists have this taste for desert landscapes. Some are much more permissive. 'Existence is cheap!' they say. 'Why not allow everything?' For these folk, metaphysical inquiry isn't just a matter of checking boxes, but involves an examination of *how* entities exist and, for instance, which entities are more fundamental than others. Are atoms more fundamental than chairs?

In a nutshell
The area of metaphysics devoted to the study of what exists.

Why it matters
We want to understand the nature of reality. Working out what does and doesn't exist is part of that project.

Key figures
Lorraine Daston, b.1951
Hypatia, *c.*360–415 BCE
Elselijn Kingma
W. V. O. Quine, 1908–2000

Make the connection
subsistence, p.71
substance, p.82
is, p.94

Exists ✓

Does not exist ✗

medical ontology

If you hang around with clinicians enough, you may well hear the term 'ontology' being bandied about. This can be confusing if you also have philosophical training. Physicians and metaphysicians typically mean something quite different by the word 'ontology'.

In healthcare and medical research, ontology refers to the way medical concepts are organized. An ontology is, essentially, a list of entities that certain practitioners are particularly interested in. Unlike metaphysicians, clinicians aren't issuing claims about the structure of reality. A medical ontology is a framework that can be shared to allow different clinicians to talk to each other and integrate data. For instance, according to different biomedical ontologies, the word 'gum' refers to a part of the mouth, a dietary substance and a type of drug preparation. Researchers need to know which ontology their collaborators are using in order to make sense of these potentially confusing terms.

Ironically, while medical ontologies are intended to facilitate communication, the dual use of the term 'ontology' can itself create unintentional obstacles. It is now common academic practice for philosophers to team up with researchers outside their discipline. Technical terms like 'ontology' can be stumbling blocks to productive discussions in this context. A medic would be confused by an atomist who claimed that their ontology only included atoms.

In a nutshell
In the context of medicine, 'ontology' refers to an organizing system of medical phenomena or concepts.

Why it matters
Sharing medical ontologies allows physicians to integrate data from different projects.

Key figures
Havi Carel, b.1971
Rachel Cooper, b.1974
Michel Foucault, 1926–1984
Drew Leder

Make the connection
biological, p.24
sex, p.36
substance, p.82

conjunction

Not far from Birmingham in the UK is a tangle of overpasses and underpasses fondly referred to as 'Spaghetti Junction'. A junction is a point where things intersect. In grammar and linguistics, a 'conjunction' is a word that joins phrases and clauses together. 'And' is one of the most common conjunctions, linking phrases *and* clauses *and* words together.

In formal logic, a conjunction serves a similar purpose, joining different statements or propositions. In order to work out whether or not a combination of statements is true (i.e., to determine its 'truth value'), it's necessary to consider conjunctions. For instance, my declaration that 'The sky is cloudy *and* it is raining' is only true if the sky is cloudy *and* it is raining. If it's cloudy, but not raining – or vice versa, or if it is neither – then the declaration is false.

Because logicians enjoy reducing ordinary language to symbols, they typically represent conjunctions using a pointy little hill, '∧', called a 'wedge'. The declaration above can be represented as two propositions (A) and (B), connected by a conjunction. In formal logic, we can write the declaration 'It is raining and the sky is cloudy' as 'A ∧ B'. This is true only when *both* of the propositions (A and B) are true. If one or other, or both of them are false, then A ∧ B is false.

In a nutshell
A conjunction is a joining word, symbolized in formal logic by a pointy little hill.

Why it matters
Conjunctions are linguistic building blocks that allow us to articulate complex thoughts.

Key figures
Ruth Barcan Marcus, 1921–2012
Dorothy Edgington, b.1941
Saul Kripke, b.1940
Alfred Tarski, 1901–1983

Make the connection
induction, p.60
validity, p.72
a priori, p.80

It's cloudy AND it's raining

disjunction

Disorder, displeasure, distasteful. The Latin prefix *dis* is a rejection of the word that follows. Disorder is not order, but the absence of order. A disjunction is, like a conjunction, a grammatical unit, used in complex sentences to express a relation between phrases and clauses. However, while conjunctions join together, disjunctions push apart. 'Or' is a common disjunction and in formal logic is usually symbolized by a 'v' (an inverted wedge).

The disjunction of two propositions is true if at least one of the individual propositions is true. If both of them are false, then the compound statement is also false.

Imagine peering through a dirty window, trying to determine what the weather is like outside. 'It's raining or the sun is shining,' you say (it's a *very* dirty window). If it *isn't* raining and the sun *isn't* shining, then I'm afraid your assessment is false. If it's raining, but not sunny (or vice versa), then your statement is true. If it's both sunny and raining, then it's also true. In formal logic, this could be written as Q v P, where 'Q' stands for the statement 'The sun is shining.'

These formal techniques are helpful when assessing the strength of an argument. If you can render the argument's premises in formal logic, assessing the conjunctions and disjunctions therein, then you have a better chance of working out if the argument is true or false.

In a nutshell
A disjunction is a logical connective, stating that at least one of two statements is true.

Why it matters
Like conjunctions, disjunctions are linguistic building blocks that allow us to capture complex thoughts.

Key figures
Gottlob Frege, 1848–1925
Jaako Hintikka, 1929–2015
Linda Zagzebski, b.1946

Make the connection
false, p.12
soundness, p.73
analysis, p.84

It's raining OR it's sunny

phenomenology

At this precise moment, I'm sitting at a desk in my room, tapping away on the keyboard. I feel slightly apprehensive about this section because 'phenomenology' is a tricky subject and hard to explain. I'm also feeling acutely conscious of time passing. I have a deadline I'm trying to meet. These are features of my experience of writing; they are part of the 'phenomenology' of this process.

Phenomenology is a philosophical approach that focuses on, and analyses, human consciousness and the structures of experience. It is the study of experiential phenomena, and as such emphasizes a careful examination of immediate, first-person experience. Its interest is in the subjective world rather than some objective, neutrally viewed reality. Phenomenologists tend to bracket questions about the existence of the external world.

The activist-scholar Sara Ahmed draws heavily on phenomenological method when she writes about her and other people's experiences of institutional racism. Understanding how institutions exclude certain groups, and how racially minoritized people are oppressed and dominated in these places, involves (Ahmed argues) an examination of the phenomenology of institutional spaces. In *Living a Feminist Life* (2017), she describes the feeling, the experience, of walking into a seminar room or a lecture hall and being surrounded by 'a sea of whiteness'. She isn't just interested in a conceptual analysis of the structures; she argues that the affective dimension of institutional racism (how it makes you feel) is just as significant.

In a nutshell
The study of human consciousness and experience.

Why it matters
How a situation feels can be just as important as its 'material reality'.

Key figures
Sara Ahmed
Hannah Arendt, 1906–1975
Edmund Husserl, 1859–1938
Emmanuel Levinas, 1906–1995

Make the connection
mood, p.29
existence, p.70
intentionality, p.129
agency, p.147

I can smell the coffee.

existentialism

Existentialism, like phenomenology, is a philosophical and literary movement that emerged in the twentieth century in mainland Europe. Like the phenomenologists, existentialists explore the subjective experience of existence, emphasizing the importance of personal responsibility, authenticity and meaning-making.

Consider again the act of writing. Facing a blank page, I am struck by its openness. I think: *I could write literally anything*. I am confronted, an existentialist would say, by a kind of radical freedom.

It can be overwhelming and writers, who can be quite inward-looking people, often write about the anxiety they experience in the writing process. When you're in complete control, there is a responsibility to be authentic, to confront difficult thoughts and feelings. How true are these sentences – how reflective are they of what I really, truly believe – and what exactly *do* I believe? Writing can generate what is called 'existential angst', an unease that arises from such musings about truth, authenticity and responsibility.

For the existentialist, there is no predetermined fixed essence that defines human purpose or nature. We are radically free. We exist, then determine what our essence may be (hence the dictum 'Existence precedes essence'). The phenomenologist's project is a descriptive one, identifying features of experience. The existentialist's project is more deliberative; through self-reflection we make meaning for ourselves, based on what we take to be our most authentic way of being.

In a nutshell
Existentialists argue that individuals create meaning through their actions.

Why it matters
Existentialism underscores the importance of individual freedom and responsibility.

Key figures
Simone de Beauvoir, 1908–1986
Albert Camus, 1913–1960
Lewis R. Gordon
Jean-Paul Sartre, 1905–1980

Make the connection
autonomy, p.146
inescapability, p.148
indeterminism, p.130

aesthetic

If you told me that my new jacket is aesthetically pleasing, I would wholeheartedly agree. It is. It's turquoise with orange zips. It has adjustable cuffs, which I think look really snazzy.

'Aesthetic' refers to matters of art, beauty or taste. If you find my new jacket aesthetically pleasing (snazzy), you're appreciating (taking pleasure in) the way it looks, the exquisite contrast of the turquoise and orange and the over-abundance of pockets.

The term 'aesthetic' is also used more generally to describe visual qualities – of a painting, for instance – or a design or an overall appearance. 'The aesthetic of the film was amazing,' you might say. 'It was so dark and grainy, and claustrophobic!' Or it can be used to talk about someone's sense of style: 'I love your aesthetic, it's so steam-punk!'

Aesthetics is the branch of philosophy that explores questions about art, beauty and taste. Are there objective standards of taste? Is it simply a *fact* that Toni Morrison's writing is better than John Grisham's? What exactly can count as 'art'? A painting? A film? An upturned urinal? An unmade bed?

In recent years, once-staid aesthetic discussions in academic philosophy have expanded to include the aesthetics of computer games and the formal aesthetics of stand-up comedy. There may be questions about what counts as 'art', but philosophers are becoming much more open when it comes to aesthetic investigations.

In a nutshell
Aesthetics examines cultural products and cultural appreciation.

Why it matters
Engaging with culture is a distinctively human activity, and one to be celebrated and explored.

Key figures
Ta–Nehisi Coates, b.1975
Susanne Langer, 1895–1985
C. Thi Nguyen
Sylvia Wynter, b.1928

Make the connection
pleasure, p.22
ideology, p.66

ascetic

An ascetic is someone who practises self-discipline and abstains from indulgence, with the aim of achieving a higher spiritual or moral goal. Think of hermits living in the desert, surviving on cactus water. Think of nuns and monks living their cloistered lives, taking vows of silence and practising celibacy. Think of religious communities that forgo technology and contact with the outside world, living off the land without TV, internet or takeaways.

Asceticism is practised in many religious and spiritual traditions and typically relates to the idea of purification. For the ascetic, the material world – the world we live in – is filled with all manner of sinful indulgences and tainting influences. In order to focus on the spiritual realm, it is best to separate yourself as much as possible from the material one.

Of course, not all ascetics are religious or spiritual. Anyone can be said to live an 'ascetic existence' if they impose restrictions on the kinds of pleasures they allow themselves to enjoy or practise intense self-discipline.

They may have a similar spelling, but aesthetic and ascetic have very different meaning. One relates to matters of taste and beauty, the other to self-discipline and abstinence. They aren't contradictory, however, and it's more than possible for somewhere or someone to have an 'ascetic aesthetic' – think of the minimalist architecture of abbey cloisters.

In a nutshell
Asceticism is characterized by self-discipline, abstinence and the renunciation of worldly pleasures.

Why it matters
Implicit in asceticism is a critique of materialism (and consumerism and commodification).

Key figures
Hipparchia, *c.*350–280 BCE
Mahavira, *c.*599–527 BCE
Julian of Norwich, *c.*1342–1416

Make the connection
pleasure, p.22
cynicism, p.101
materialism, p.124

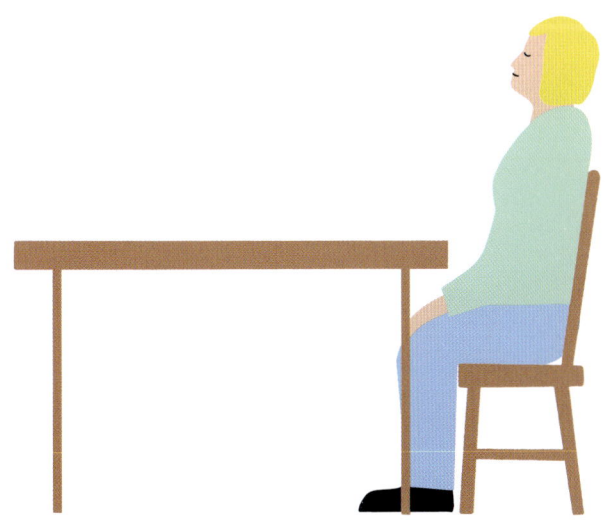

semantics

'That's just semantics!' Such declarations are normally accompanied by a frustrated roll of the eyes. The thought is that the disagreement is simply a disagreement over terms. The speakers aren't *actually* in conflict, they're just using the same words differently.

Semantics is the branch of linguistics that deals with meaning: what do words and phrases mean, and how is that meaning conveyed? In some ways, this book is intended to help mitigate such semantic disagreements. For instance, the section on 'identity' explores the different meanings of the word and the confusions that arise when these meanings get muddled. But semantics isn't just about how a word is defined, it's about the relationship between linguistic signs (such as the words on a page) and the concepts to which they refer (the 'referents'). It deals with the way meaning is communicated within a language system, including the influence of intention, gesture and other social factors.

Imagine overhearing two people disagreeing about the idea of a 'free society'. One of them thinks there should be minimal state intervention. The other thinks a free society needs a hands-on government to address systemic inequalities. The disagreement is partly semantic. 'Freedom' can be the ability to act without interference but, in a broader context, social freedom requires equal opportunities, which, in turn, require government intervention. Semantic consideration of the word 'freedom' conjures up these different thoughts and widens the scope of an argument.

In a nutshell
The study of meaning, exploring how words convey specific ideas in different contexts.

Why it matters
Semantics is a discipline that attempts to understand how we understand each other.

Key figures
Roland Barthes, 1915–1980
Umberto Eco, 1932–2016
Julia Kristeva, b.1941
Ferdinand de Saussure, 1857–1913

Make the connection
knowledge, p.8
rhetoric, p.150

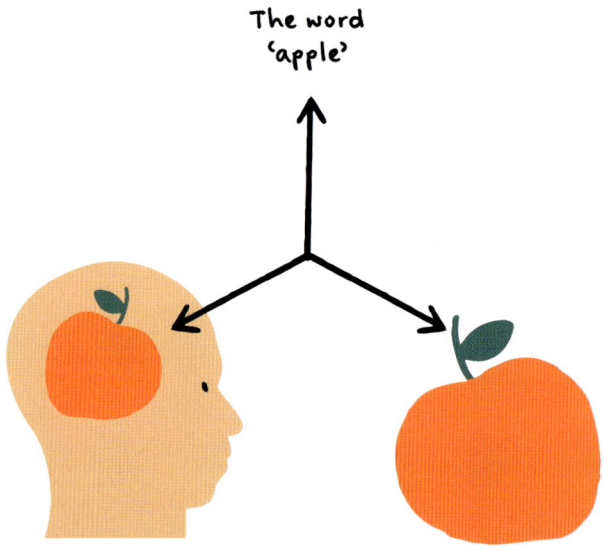

The word 'apple'

hermeneutics

Hermeneutics is sometimes called the art of interpretation. It is a theoretical approach that analyses texts, language and other forms of symbolic expression in a way that extends beyond the literal definition of terms.

Someone could, for instance, conduct a hermeneutic analysis of the above section on semantics. It would consider the literary devices I've used to discuss the subject (e.g., the examples). It would also consider your position, as a reader interpreting the text. Why are you reading it in the first place? What do you hope to glean? My own role would be examined. Why am I writing this book? Why am I writing in the first-person? Do I have a political or cultural agenda?

Semantics and hermeneutics consider how signs and symbols connect to concepts and create meaning. Hermeneutics, however, is particularly interested in the *oblique* connections, the meaning beyond literal definitions. A hermeneutic analysis of my use of the first person might consider the academic preference for the passive voice. My inclusion of myself ('I', 'my') in this book isn't a literal or explicit criticism of depersonalized academic texts, but it may be a device used to imply my wariness around such ways of writing. Semantics concerns itself with the study of linguistic meaning, while hermeneutics is a more holistic approach, focused on political context, material reality and intention.

In a nutshell
The study of interpretation.

Why it matters
Awareness of hermeneutic phenomena allows us to read 'subtext'.

Key figures
Hans-Georg Gadamer, 1900–2002
Paula Moya
Paul Ricoeur, 1913–2005

Make the connection
rational, p.14
sarcasm, p.30
power, p.41

The art of interpretation

materialism

When Madonna sang, 'We are living in a material world, and I am a material girl', she was offering an acerbic commentary on consumer culture. In this 'material world', everything can be bought: fast cars, big TVs, happiness, even love. However, her lyrics could also be the slogan for a metaphysical thesis known as materialism, which holds that only material things can really be said to exist.

The metaphysical materialist holds that we are living in a material world, and that we are all material people. Everything is material, in that everything that exists is constituted by, and can ultimately be explained in terms of, physical entities and their properties.

Throughout history, philosophers have posited the existence of various immaterial substances, like souls, ghosts, angels, gods and demons. Many of these entities were once used to explain phenomena that are now (due to the insights of science) explicable in exclusively material terms. Why would we explain volcanoes by invoking a god's fury if we have comprehensive geological information about plate tectonics? The materialist's answer is that we shouldn't.

The situation becomes more complicated when we consider everyday immaterial objects such as thoughts. Imagine an ice cream. Is this imaginary ice cream material or not? The materialist will use neurological science (for instance) to explain a mental phenomenon. But is the human mind really just the by-product of synapses firing?

In a nutshell
The view that only material things exist.

Why it matters
Materialism runs counter to much religious belief, which supposes the existence of immaterial substances, including gods and angels.

Key figures
Robert Boyle,
1627–1691
Margaret Cavendish,
1623–1673
Democritus,
c.460–370 BCE
Valerie Gray
Hardcastle

Make the connection
scientific, p.96
ontology, p.114
particle theory, p.140

Only material things exist.

physicalism

To quote from another classic '80s anthem: 'Let's get physical!' Olivia Newton-John's 1981 smash hit uses 'physical' to imply bodily action (specifically, physical intimacy). It's the same use that we find in the phrase 'Physical Education'. But 'physicalism' wouldn't be taught in PE class. It's not about muscles or how much you can bench-press. Physicalism refers to a philosophical and ideological position. Physicalists hold that everything that exists is fundamentally physical. In this sense, it is very similar to materialism.

Where it departs from materialism is in its purview. Physicalists don't limit themselves to traditional material substances such as particles. The physicalist's ontology (their call sheet of existing things) admits all entities and properties recognized by physics, which may extend beyond what is traditionally considered 'material' to include fields and forces like gravity, which aren't as easily apprehended as hard matter.

Physicalism gained prominence in the twentieth century, reflecting advances in physics and a more flexible approach to ontological analysis. Physicalism can, perhaps, be said to be a broader position than materialism. Materialism can be seen as a subset of physicalism, though materialists (predictably) would probably want to argue the opposite. Still, most people (or perhaps most philosophers) use the terms interchangeably, without attending to historical and contextual factors.

In a nutshell
The view that only physical things exist.

Why it matters
Physicalists argue against the existence of immaterial substances like ghosts, but they leave room in their ontology for physical forces.

Key figures
Patricia Churchland, b.1943
Jaegwon Kim, 1934–2019
Ruth Millikan, b.1933
Hilary Putnam, 1926–2016

Make the connection
effect, p.20
substratum, p.82
epiphenomenalism, p.153

behaviourism

Yesterday on my way to work, I cycled by a man trimming his garden hedge. He didn't look like he was enjoying it very much. He was scowling while viciously chopping at the privet.

Some people think that the best way to understand behaviour is to think about a person's mental state. What was this guy feeling? Was he angry? Behaviourists, by contrast, think his presentation would be best and most reliably understood, not by trying to delve into his subjective experience, but through observation.

Behaviourism is a psychological theory that originated in the early twentieth century and that emphasizes the study of observable and measurable behaviours as the focus of psychological inquiry. Mental processes and subjective experiences, which are harder (if not impossible) to accurately measure, are left out of behavioural analysis.

The hedge-cutter's actions, for example, can be understood as a response to environmental stimuli. Maybe the sight of a messy hedge prompted the hedge-cutting behaviour. Maybe this stimulus was further encouraged by negative reinforcement (e.g., scolding from his spouse). We might offer other theories about the man's scowl depending on other observations. Maybe he just has a scowly face.

The behaviourist's focus is on observable behaviours and the environmental factors that contribute to such behaviours.

In a nutshell
The view that psychological investigation should focus on observable behaviour rather than internal mental states.

Why it matters
Behaviourism provides an alternative model for psychological inquiry, bypassing the tricky business of internal mental states.

Key figures
R. M. Hare, 1919–2002
Iris Murdoch, 1919–1999
Ivan Pavlov, 1849–1936
B. F. Skinner, 1904–1990

Make the connection
indeterminism, p.130
agency, p.147

behaviouralism

Behaviouralism is, essentially, behaviourism transposed into the political sphere. It focuses on the observable actions and behaviours of individuals and groups in political and social contexts. It is concerned, primarily, with the systematic study of political behaviour, eschewing abstract theories and ideologies.

Consider voter turn-out. Whether or not voters go to the polling stations depends on a stimulus, such as the announcement of an upcoming election, and its response, i.e., the decision whether or not to participate in the election. Behaviouralists will be interested in the positive reinforcement offered to voters (e.g., a focus on the importance of civic responsibility) as well as the negative (potential dissatisfaction with the elected candidate if you don't vote). Behaviouralists will also consider environmental influences. Voting behaviour can be affected by, for instance, the accessibility of polling locations and the ease of voter registration.

Behaviouralists aren't concerned with mental states or rational deliberation. They're interested in seeing which stimuli prompt which responses, and the resulting statistical trends. This information can then, in turn, be utilized by politicians and their campaign managers. If it's clear that candidates with strong social-media platforms do better than those without, that's sufficient reason for aspiring politicians to increase their social-media presence. It doesn't matter what the electorate are *actually* thinking. What matters is a clear correlation between a stimulus and a response.

In a nutshell
An approach to political analysis, focusing on statistical likelihoods.

Why it matters
Campaigners working with behaviouralist models tend to be less interested in morality and justice than in what stimuli will be successful.

Key figures
Anthony Downs, 1930–2021
Stanley Milgram, 1933–1984
Kwame Nkrumah, 1909–1972

Make the connection

POLLING STATION

intention

Before I start writing, I compose a sentence in my head with the aim of typing it out on my keyboard. I form an intention to write, then I commit to doing it. I lift my hands, press my fingertips to the keys. The result is an action, of which you're seeing the result.

The ability to form intentions is a complex cognitive process associated with the capacity for decision-making, goal-directed behaviour and agency. The ability to form intentions is often thought to be a crucial aspect for conscious decision-making and, relatedly, free will. If I weren't able to form an intention to write a sentence and I just wrote spontaneously or automatically, then I wouldn't have *chosen* the course of action. I wouldn't be writing freely.

While intentions appear to be a necessary ingredient for free actions, it's unclear that they are themselves freely formed.

The philosopher Gregory Kavka explored the links between intentions, rationality and decision-making in a thought experiment known as 'the toxin puzzle'. Imagine a millionaire offered you a large financial reward to swallow a relatively harmless toxin in a few hours' time (don't ask why). Imagine the millionaire assures you that you don't *actually* need to swallow the toxin, you simply have to form the intention to do so. But thinking that you don't need to swallow the toxin undermines the intention to do so, no? The implication appears to be that intentions can't be stand-alone states, but require a commitment to action.

In a nutshell
An mental mechanism relating to the performance of a future action.

Why it matters
The formation of intentions is essential to conscious decision-making.

Key figures
Franz Brentano, 1838–1917
Jennifer Hornsby, b.1951
Edmund Husserl, 1859–1938

Make the connection
phenomenology, p.118
agency, p.147

intentionality

The word 'intention' comes from the Latin *intendere*, meaning 'to stretch toward' or 'to aim at'. British moral philosopher Elizabeth Anscombe explains it in relation to bows and arrows. When you draw a bow (i.e., when the bowstring is *in tension*), the arrow is to be propelled in a specific direction. Intention is the mental act of aiming, of setting your thoughts on a particular target.

In the philosophy of mind, intentionality is understood to be a property of lots of different kinds of mental states, not just of intentions. It refers to the 'aboutness' or directedness of a thought. It can be pretty much any kind of thought. If I'm thinking about a loved one, that person is the 'intentional object'. Intentionality is a quality of thinking and doesn't require the formation of intentions.

The notion of intentionality is helpful when unpicking the difference between mental states such as emotions and moods. Emotions tend to have intentional objects. If you're angry, you're angry about something. If you're in love, you're in love with someone. Moods, by contrast, don't appear to have intentional objects. If you're grumpy, your grumpiness need not have a specific focus. It can be a general malaise. It can settle on certain things, but these things aren't really the cause of the moodiness, they're just in the wrong place at the wrong time.

An intention is a mental state that involves a commitment to perform an action. Intentionality is the quality of mental states that are directed towards specific objects.

In a nutshell
A quality of thinking. It refers to the directedness, or 'aboutness', of a thought.

Why it matters
It characterizes much of our experience of the world. Our thoughts are thoughts *about* things.

Key figures
G. E. M. Anscombe, 1919–2001
Roderick Chisholm, 1916–1999
Daniel Dennett, b.1942
Maurice Merleau-Ponty, 1908–1961

Make the connection
emotion, p.28
phenomenology, p.118
agency, p.147

I'll take aim.

indeterminism

Something prompted you to start reading this book. Maybe you received it as a birthday present. Maybe your teacher has set it as a homework assignment. Perhaps you were simply bored in a bookshop and picked it up. Did you choose to do so freely? It might feel like that, but in some renderings of reality, everything we do (including reading books) is causally determined. This position is called 'determinism'.

The determinist could think that you were always going to want to read this book. Events in your childhood disposed you to have an interest in philosophy, perhaps. The fact that you're reading this sentence is just the result of a long causal chain, which stretches back in time and down to the quantum level, where particles bump into each other in predictable ways. Everything you and I do is inevitable.

The indeterminist disagrees. They reject the claim that all events and processes are strictly determined. Our futures are not already written. For the indeterminist some things are inherently unpredictable. Look at quantum mechanics, they may say, where the behaviour of particles is described by probabilities rather than certainties. We can't state what's going to happen because there's an element of randomness to reality.

Some indeterminists think this inherent uncertainty supports the claim that we have free will. Others are more circumspect. Acting randomly, they say, is not the same as acting freely.

In a nutshell
Indeterminists deny that all events are causally determined.

Why it matters
If our actions are all determined, can we really be said to be responsible for them? Free will and moral responsibility are interconnected.

Key figures
Thomas Hobbes, 1588–1679
Pierre-Simon Laplace, 1749–1827
Baruch Spinoza, 1632–1677
Susan Wolf, b.1952

Make the connection
ethics, p.39
materialism, p.124
particle theory, p.140

incompatibilism

When we say two people are incompatible, we mean they don't suit each other. There's some kind of fundamental mismatch. Incompatibilists think the same is true for determinism and free will: they just don't work.

Incompatibilists fall into two camps. Some believe all actions are causally determined. Consequently, they say, we don't have free will (they are 'incompatibilist determinists'). Others believe in causal indeterminacy; they think we can in fact act freely. Indeterminacy isn't just a matter of random behaviour (since free will is more than acting randomly). The incompatibilist *in*determinists think we have the ability to make choices that aren't causally downstream of the interactions of minuscule particles.

Incompatibilist indeterminists are sometimes called 'libertarians' (not to be confused with liberals, who are also sometimes called libertarians). Libertarians hold that individuals are self-causing agents. The fact that you're reading this book is a choice, not the by-product of your genetic inheritance or the interaction of subatomic particles. It remains an open question as to where, exactly, the ability to act freely comes from.

Not everyone is as hard-line as the incompatibilists. Some philosophers engaging in the debate argue that determinism and free will can work together. Just as a river is free when it is free to run its course, so, they argue, we are free to act when our desires, intentions and choices are unencumbered.

In a nutshell
The view that free will and determinism are incompatible.

Why it matters
Where we stand on these issues will determine our views of freedom and agency.

Key figures
Simone de Beauvoir, 1908–1986
David Hume, 1711–1776
Jean-Paul Sartre, 1905–1980
Arthur Schopenhauer, 1788–1860

Make the connection
liberalism, p.47
existentialism, p.119
agency, p.147

transhumanism

Medical science has made dramatic advances in the last hundred or so years. If you have a dicky heart, then a pacemaker can be fitted. All manner of scanners and monitors now offer unparalleled insight into the inner workings of the human body. Not only is technology used to ameliorate health conditions, it can be used to proactively enhance our lives. Genetic manipulation has created more reproductive possibilities. A child can inherit genetic material from three, rather than two, parents. Such scientific achievements are technically impressive, but they have also altered the ethical landscape and created new moral conundrums.

Transhumanists believe that the use of technology to enhance human physical and cognitive capabilities should be encouraged. The transhumanist movement is optimistic about technology's ability to help us overcome biological limitations and generally improve the human condition. If scientists can create a prosthetic arm to assist an amputee, why can't they develop prostheses to improve, rather than simply to mitigate harm? Wouldn't it be great to have three arms? The goal is to augment human capacities, but transhumanists are also aware of the ethical pitfalls of doing so, and don't necessarily endorse enhancement wholesale.

One significant worry with the transhumanist project is the reliance on corporations for the production of this technology. As we know from any number of dystopian science-fiction stories, if human enhancement is tied to money-making ventures, the result might well be an acute worsening of social disparities.

In a nutshell
Transhumanists are enthusiastic about human enhancement through technology.

Why it matters
Implicit to much transhumanist thought is the idea that humans can be improved. The flip side of this is the thought that some humans may be 'deficient'.

Key figures
Nick Bostrom, b.1973
Donna Haraway, b.1944
N. Katherine Hayles, b.1943
Carl Sagan, 1934–1996

Make the connection
natural, p.25
substance, p.83
scientistic, p.97

Human technological enhancement

posthumanism

Posthumanism has a broader purview than transhumanism. Posthumanist thinkers are interested in the effects of technology on the idea of humanity. They aren't necessarily interested in enhancement; their focus is on the way enhancements blur the boundary of what counts as human and what as machine.

The blurriness that results from technological intervention in the human troubles the ideological position known as humanism. Humanism refers to the traditional focus on human perspectives – on the importance of individuals and on their rational capacities. Posthumanism blurs the discrete boundaries that humanists draw around human beings, emphasizing how deeply enmeshed we are with technology, the environment and other non-human entities.

Consider the voting process in an election. The humanist's aim might be to ensure that each individual citizen is free and unhindered in registering their vote. This means, perhaps, minimizing the political influence of social-media platforms, as well as reducing the number and influence of non-human actors, like bots. The posthumanist will recognize these dangers, but will emphasize, too, how the internet has already moved us beyond the humanist ideal of a discrete, individual agent. Voting (the posthumanist might say) is a networked and collective activity, involving human votes *and* technological systems, algorithms and interconnected social networks. Posthumanists aren't interested in humans – they're interested in the entanglement of human organism, technology and the environment.

In a nutshell
An intellectual movement that challenges many of the strict boundaries drawn by humanism.

Why it matters
Posthumanism offers a nuanced understanding of the role of technology in human life.

Key figures
Rosi Braidotti, b.1954
N. Katherine Hayles, b.1943
Ray Kurzweil, b.1948
Bruno Latour, 1947–2022

Make the connection
biological, p.24
existence, p.70
postmodernism, p.110

What's a human? What's a machine?

normal

What do we mean when we say something is 'normal'? There's an assumption that the word simply means 'common', 'typical' or 'usual'. 'That's completely normal behaviour for a two-year-old' might mean 'Don't worry about the screaming infant, all two-year-olds go through a tantrum phase.' In a statistical sense, the average height of individuals in a population is considered the 'normal' height, or the 'norm'.

But the word 'normal' isn't only used to capture statistical likelihood. It can be a value judgement as well. When people say that heterosexuality is normal, the implication isn't just that it's common, but that it's the right way to be. Correspondingly, then, other sexualities are 'abnormal', which doesn't just mean that they're rare (which they clearly aren't), but that they're wrong. In this way, 'normal' often overlaps with the term 'natural', used to describe both what *is* the case and what *ought* to be the case.

A 'norm' is a shared, expected or standard pattern of behaviour or belief within a group. Norms provide guidelines for 'appropriate' behaviour in order to facilitate social interactions. For instance, in England it is the norm to expel nasal detritus into a small piece of linen or thin paper (sometimes called 'blowing your nose'), whereas the norm in other countries might be to expel it onto the street. There are different norms in different societies, and individuals are expected to conform to these differing standards of behaviour.

In a nutshell
Normalcy can refer to what is common, but also what is seen to be 'natural'.

Why it matters
Claims about normalcy can be used to disempower some 'abnormal' groups and privilege others.

Key figures
Pierre Bourdieu, 1930–2002
Darren Chetty, b.1972
Adrienne Keene, b.1985
Adrienne Rich, 1929–2012

Make the connection
reasonable, p.15
natural, p.25
ideology, p.66

normative

The word 'normal' comes from the Latin *normalis*, which was originally used in the context of carpentry to mean 'made according to a standard or a rule'. It captures the notion of a *standard* (of behaviour) and of something *being standard* (common). Importantly, it also has an instructional element: 'You should do this in order to do that.'

Normative statements or approaches express views about what is right or wrong, desirable or undesirable, and in some sense what *ought* to be standard practice. Such statements are prescriptive. They prescribe certain actions and proscribe others. While the word 'normal' can be used in a descriptive sense, to describe what is typical, 'normative' doesn't indicate whether or not something is common. Consider, for instance, the following normative statement: 'It is morally wrong to deceive or lie to others.' There's nothing inconsistent about saying this in a society where honesty is vanishingly rare.

Normally, we use 'normal' descriptively, to describe what is usual, and we use 'normative' prescriptively, to refer to values or to reflect judgements about what is right or acceptable. Of course, since they share a linguistic root, there is overlap (as we've seen, 'normal' is often a value judgement). But don't worry, this kind of semantic blurriness is all completely normal.

In a nutshell
Normativity refers to standards that prescribe what ought to be.

Why it matters
This concept allows us to understand how social power is exerted.

Key figures
Emmanuel Chukwudi Eze, 1963–2007
Alicia Garza, b.1981
Antonio Gramsci, 1891–1937
Shirley Anne Tate, b.1956

Make the connection
hegemony, p.67
prescriptive, p.74
objective, p.77

double consciousness

Sociologist W. E. B. Du Bois developed the concept of double consciousness to describe the psychological challenge of viewing oneself simultaneously from two opposing perspectives. Writing in the nineteenth and twentieth centuries, Du Bois documented and theorized the experiences of African-American people in a white supremacist society, specifically the United States.

According to Du Bois' analysis, a Black American man will have an internal sense of himself – a complex, multifaceted understanding of his own hopes, desires, fears and worries. Unfortunately, this sense of selfhood will run up against, conflict with or be undermined by racist social stories told about Black American men, which deny them personhood and rich inner lives (among many other things). There is a clash, a cognitive dissonance.

When you believe yourself to be one thing and society tells you that you're something else, you can experience an acute internal tension, a split in your identity. This split is double consciousness. For Du Bois, it is a consequence of systemic racism and prejudice.

The disparity between these two perspectives needs to be navigated, and those on the receiving end of racism are forced to engage with – and to a certain extent *internalize* – racist ideas and depictions of Black people. Double consciousness creates an obstacle to self-understanding and an unhindered sense of an authentic self.

In a nutshell
The split sense of self that results from living in a social world that neglects or actively attacks your humanity.

Why it matters
The term captures a central tension experienced by marginalized groups living within supremacist societies.

Key figures
W. E. B. Du Bois, 1868–1963
Frantz Fanon, 1925–1961
Toni Morrison, 1931–2019
Gayatri Spivak, b.1942

Make the connection
race, p.42
misogyny, p.49
prejudice, p.50

consciousness raising

It's possible that double consciousness may be mitigated by something called 'consciousness raising'. Gaining prominence in the feminist movements of the 1960s, consciousness raising is a process of increasing awareness and understanding of social and political issues, including white supremacy and patriarchal domination.

The aim of consciousness raising is to foster collective empowerment through education and discussion. The term evokes the Marxist notion of 'false consciousness'. Some groups are led to hold false beliefs by more powerful members of society. These beliefs, which constitute false consciousness, are contrary to the group's self-interest; women, for example, are poorly served by the belief that 'a woman's place is in the home'. Consciousness raising addresses such mistaken beliefs (including racist, homophobic, ableist and misogynistic attitudes) by analysing them within the broader social context. The aim is to uncover patterns, systemic issues and shared concerns in the hope of building solidarity.

Consciousness raising is a general political strategy used to empower people through education. Learning more about the ideology of white supremacy – which benefits white people at the cost of people of colour – can clarify the tension inherent in double consciousness. Because it involves group action and shared understanding, consciousness raising can also help challenge the view of social attitudes (including racist ones) as those shared by all members of society.

In a nutshell
A political project focused on spreading public awareness of systemic issues.

Why it matters
In order to combat unjust systems it is necessary to be aware of them.

Key figures
Alicia Garza, b.1981
Roxane Gay, b.1974
Rosa Luxembourg, 1871–1919
Kate Manne, b.1983

Make the connection
hegemony, p.67
consciousness, p.88
socialism, p.93

gnostic

The Greek *gnosis* means 'insight'. The word 'Gnostic' shares this root with a number of everyday terms, like diagnosis and prognosis. 'Prognosis', for example, is insight gleaned in advance (a prediction).

Gnosticism refers to a collection of European philosophical traditions that emerged in the first few centuries of the Common Era. The Gnostic belief systems, which are many and varied, are characterized by an emphasis on acquiring spiritual knowledge as a means of salvation, and a belief that this spiritual knowledge is in some way secret and the preserve of a special few (the Gnostics).

Most Gnostic systems view the material world as flawed, even malevolent, and believe that individuals can find their way into a higher, divine, spiritual realm by gaining access to esoteric knowledge. In some sense, then, the Gnostics were exclusionary in their beliefs – a members-only club. At the same time, Gnostic groups often rejected the authority of mainstream religious institutions, including organized forms of Christianity. There is a particular focus in Gnosticism on direct personal experience and knowledge of the divine, rather than on rituals and hierarchical structures. In this sense, Gnosticism might be seen to be more open and democratic than mainstream religious systems.

Gnostic ideas surfaced more recently, in New Age thought of the mid-twentieth century, where there is a similar focus on mystical and transcendent experiences and esoteric teachings.

In a nutshell
Refers to a spiritual tradition that emphasizes secret, esoteric knowledge.

Why it matters
While there are few self-proclaimed Gnostics these days, similar attitudes characterize certain forms of political engagement (think, for instance, of the Q-Anon conspiracy theorists).

Key figures
L. Ron Hubbard, 1911–1986
Marcion of Sinope, 85–160 CE
Valentinus, *c.*100–160 CE

Make the connection
knowledge, p.8
power, p.41
suspicion, p.57

agnostic

The prefix *a* means 'not', or 'without', so 'agnostic' means without insight, or without knowledge. In the context of religious belief, an agnostic is someone who is uncertain about the existence of God. Where theists believe in God's existence and atheists determinedly don't, the agnostic shrugs their shoulders and says, 'I don't know!' This might be because they think certain metaphysical questions are beyond the scope of human understanding, or it might be that they simply haven't spent much time thinking about it.

While agnosticism is most commonly associated with religious belief, it can apply more broadly, too: for instance to metaphysical questions about the nature of reality. You can be an agnostic about scientific theories, ethics and morality, and about knowledge in general ('I don't know what I know!'). Agnosticism is a recognition of the limits of our human understanding.

In contrast to the Gnostic, who believes we – or at least some of us – can access secret, spiritual knowledge of reality, the agnostic is sceptical about our ability to understand the world and our place within it. There is modesty here (which is relatively unusual in philosophical discourse). 'Sometimes,' says the agnostic, 'we simply can't know, or work out, the answers to these Big Questions. Sometimes the philosophical puzzles are intractable. It's nobody's fault, we just have to reconcile ourselves to not knowing.'

In a nutshell
Typically refers to someone who isn't sure whether or not a higher power (or some other unevidenced entity) exists.

Why it matters
If you think religion and religious belief are important, then you'll likely think the existence of God or gods is important too.

Key figures
Ayaan Hirsi Ali, b.1969
Thomas Huxley, 1825–1895
William James, 1842–1910
Bertrand Russell, 1872–1970

Make the connection
belief, p.9
scepticism, p.56
cynicism, p.101

particle theory

I've never been any good at snooker, but I understand the principles of the game. You use a ball (the cue ball) to hit other balls, which go into pockets or bounce into the cushions, then other balls, and everything bounces around in law-ordained ways. This is also how I conceive of particle theory, a scientific model used to describe the properties and behaviour of material things.

The central premise is that all matter is composed of tiny particles that bounce around, knocking other tiny particles, and then others, according to specific physical laws. Before scientists developed the technology to directly observe the microscopic realm, philosophers posited the existence of these minuscule building blocks: atoms, molecules or (to use a seventeenth-century term) 'corpuscles'.

All matter is composed of these extremely small particles and they move around constantly, pushed by changing temperatures and pressures. Through reference to particles, scientists can explain material changes. For instance, the melting of a wax candle can be explained by an increase in temperature, which increases the movement of the wax particles and weakens the bonds between them.

Many materialists are also particle theorists. They believe that only matter exists, that there are no souls or other immaterial substances. Some of the materialists –'mereological nihilists' – even go so far as to say that only tiny particles exist. It seems that there are chairs and tables and the like, but these are really just bundles of particles.

In a nutshell
A scientific model that explains physical phenomena by invoking tiny particles.

Why it matters
This theory is fundamental to modern conceptions of physics.

Key figures
Robert Boyle, 1627–1692
John Locke, 1632–1704
Damaris Cudworth Masham, 1659–1708

Make the connection
identity, p.6
nihilism, p.86
ontology, p.114
materialism, p.124

particularism

Particle theory isn't particularly particularist. In modern physics and chemistry, particle theory is taken to apply across the board. Its principles are principles for everything, with no exceptions. All matter is composed of particles and all particles abide by the same physical laws. Particularism, by contrast, is a rejection of the application of universal principles. It emphasizes the importance of context and particular circumstances.

Ethical particularism rejects the application of universal moral principles. Take honesty, for instance. Some people think we should always be honest, regardless of the circumstances. 'But wait,' says the particularist. 'What about situations where a lie might save a life?' Imagine an axe-wielding villain is searching for your granny and asks where she's hiding. Surely in this very particular circumstance you should lie? For the particularist, universal principles are too rigid. It's not possible to develop any meaningful (rather than uselessly broad) instructions for ethical living. Instead, the particularist focusses on ethical engagement. Ethics isn't merely a matter of following rules, it requires us to be sensitive to the nuances of an encounter, and to be able to respond to it appropriately. Of course, some people may say that particularism is itself a generalized approach to ethics, but such people are, perhaps, simply being particularly particular.

In a nutshell
The rejection of the universal application of, for example, ethical theories.

Why it matters
This theory allows for nuanced and flexible engagement with moral concerns.

Key figures
G. E. M Anscombe, 1919–2001
Iris Murdoch, 1919–1999
Bernard Williams, 1929–2003

Make the connection

idealism

Calling someone an 'idealist' implies that they have high-minded, noble and quite possibly unrealistic expectations. This is the most common usage of the term 'idealist' in day-to-day life. It refers to a mindset in which the aim is perfection and anything less is considered a failure. In metaphysics, however, idealism is more about ideas than ideals. It is the view that mental entities and modes (thoughts, ideas, concepts, consciousnesses) are metaphysically more fundamental than material things.

Materialists argue that there is an external world, independent of human thought and action. Were humans and other sentient beings to suddenly pop out of existence, reality would be largely unchanged. Idealists, by contrast, think that reality is in some way *constituted* by thought.

There are various forms of metaphysical idealism. For some, the material world exists because it is perceived by conscious minds (hence the Latin dictum *Esse est percipi*, or 'To be is to be perceived'). For others, sometimes referred to as 'transcendental idealists', there is an external, independent realm, but it is one we cannot access. To some degree, for these thinkers, we live in a world of our own making. Others argue that reality is in fact a dynamic, interconnected system of ideas, a manifestation of some kind of mega-mind or world-spirit. Views differ, but the central thought is that thought is central.

In a nutshell
Without minds, there wouldn't be anything else either.

Why it matters
Idealism, like many metaphysical theses, becomes particularly relevant in religious discourse (for instance, is reality dependent on the mind of God?).

Key figures
George Berkeley, 1685–1753
Ibn Sina, 'Avicenna', c.980–1037 CE
Constance Jones, 1848–1922
Immanuel Kant, 1724–1804

Make the connection
consciousness, p.88
ontology, p.114
materialism, p.124

solipsism

Solipsism is a slightly more extreme philosophical position than idealism. It posits that only oneself – one's own mind – can truly be said to exist. Nothing else in reality is certain. There is no reliable evidence of the external world or the minds of others. In fact, there is a high chance such things may not exist at all.

Solipsism is a very lonely philosophical position. It takes subjectivity to an extreme, suggesting that one's consciousness is the only actual point of epistemic purchase. All we can know are our experiences, and these experiences (like reading this book, sitting in a chair, the taste of coffee) are not sufficiently robust sources of information. When you talk to a friend or pick up the phone or walk down the street, there is nothing, really, which can justify the thought that you're actually doing these things, rather than imagining them.

While idealism is a metaphysical thesis, solipsism is primarily an epistemic position. Idealism holds that ideas and other such mental entities are fundamental parts of reality. The solipsist insists that we can only really be sure of our own experiences (including our experiences of these mental entities) and not external reality. It's about knowledge, and about what we can and can't know about the make-up of reality.

In a nutshell
The thesis that the only thing one can be sure exists is oneself.

Why it matters
Sometimes, in order to be sure about what we know, it helps to assume a 'doubtful' solipsistic position.

Key figures
René Descartes, 1596–1650
Rae Langton, b.1961
Sextus Empiricus, c.300–200 BCE

Make the connection
scepticism, p.56
subjective, p.76
phenomenology, p.118

genetic fallacy

A lot of philosophical ideas originated with, and were developed by, rather nasty people. Aristotle was a slave owner, Immanuel Kant spent a considerable amount of his time justifying racist hierarchies, and most (if not all) philosophers in the Western canon were white men largely unbothered by the exclusion of women, non-binary folk and people of colour from the discipline. Does this mean we should reject their theories and ideas wholesale?

For some, the answer is 'no'. To reject an idea simply because its originator was a bigot may be to commit what is known as the 'genetic fallacy'. The fallacy occurs when a claim is judged to be true or false based on its origin or history, rather than on its intrinsic merits and without considering the evidence or reasoning behind the claim. 'Genetic' here relates to the Greek *gene*, meaning 'birth' or 'origin'. Just because an idea originates with a prejudiced thinker doesn't mean the idea itself is prejudicial.

Other philosophers are more circumspect. It may not be immediately clear that Kant's ideas are accented by his racism, but prejudice and bias often work in subtle and insidious ways. There may be no obvious connection between Kant's conception of rationality and his white supremacist worldview, but closer critical inspection may reveal that his understanding of rationality may privilege certain cultural, white ways of being.

In a nutshell
To commit the genetic fallacy is to dismiss or accept an argument based on its origin rather than its content.

Why it matters
Genetic fallacies are everywhere, and given the way trust functions, very easy to commit.

Key figures
Michèle le Doeuff, b.1948
Emmanuel Chukwudi Eze, 1963–2007
Evelyn Fox Keller, 1936–2023
Ernest Nagel, 1901–1985

Make the connection
natural, p.25
ought, p.95
scientistic, p.97

Bad people can have good ideas!

genealogy

'Genealogy' refers to the study of descent. A family tree, which documents family relationships, is an example of a genealogy; it is the history of a family. In philosophy, genealogy refers to the historical study of an idea. The aim of the philosophical genealogy is to trace the development and emergence of concepts, institutions or practices over time, to pick apart the different social influences that have shaped a concept or worldview.

To a certain extent, much of this book is composed of genealogical analyses. When we're looking at words and tracing their different meanings over time and how those meanings shift, we're doing genealogy. It's relevant that the term comes from a Greek word meaning 'generation'.

Importantly, genealogies aren't necessarily linear. A word (like 'ideal' or 'normal') can signify various things at the same time and these meanings can be shaped by a variety of social factors, with a variety of historical origins, and they can overlap and affect each other. As such, the aim of a genealogy is very different from the genetic analysis that underpins claims about genetic fallacies. The genealogist is not interested in a single point of origin. He or she eschews unitary, linear analysis and rejects the thought that there can be a straightforward intellectual history of ideas (e.g., Kant's conception of rationality is not really Kant's, but emerges from a mess of social and cultural relations).

In a nutshell
The study of descent.

Why it matters
Genealogies provide subtle insights into the creation of concepts.

Key figures
Michel Foucault,
1926–1984
Raymond Geuss,
b.1946
Friedrich Nietzsche,
1844–1900

Make the connection
ideology, p.66
postmodernism, p.110

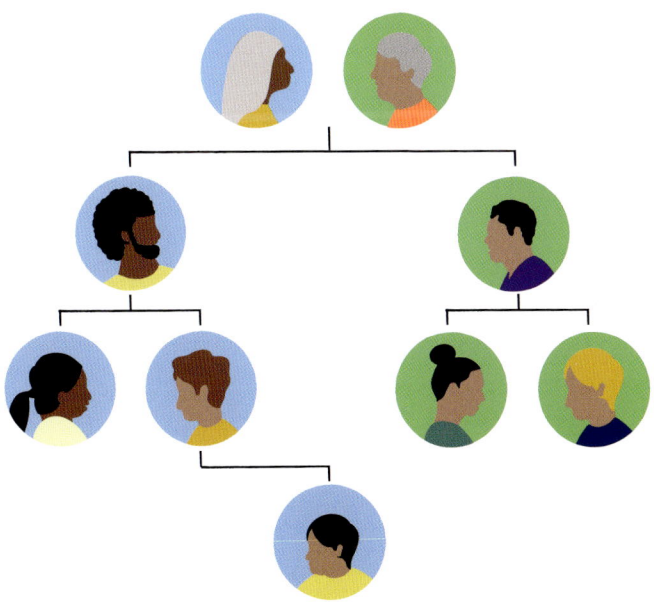

autonomy

Imagine you have no choice but to read this sentence – and the following sentence, indeed all of the sentences in this book – until you've finished the whole darn thing. Imagine I'm forcing you to read these words. You can't resist! It's a far-fetched scenario, but the point is that when someone is in control of you and your actions – when someone determines what you can and can't do, when they set the rules and terms of engagement – then something special is being damaged.

'Autonomy' comes from the Greek *autos*, meaning 'self' (like an 'autobiography', which is a biography written about oneself). *Nomos* means 'law' or 'rule' (to 'nominate' is to name someone according to an established law). 'Autonomy' refers to the capacity or condition of having the freedom and independence to make your own decisions and choices without external influence or coercion. It is the capacity to govern yourself, to abide by your own rules.

The autonomy of the individual is a central strut of many democratic institutions. For example, citizens are expected to act autonomously, to be free from coercion, when they're voting for elected officials. Autonomy – self-governance – is the basis for much of modern law, which situates responsibility with individuals. If someone is autonomous, then they're in control of themselves and are the ultimate authors of their actions.

In a nutshell
The right or condition of self-government, either for individuals or for groups.

Why it matters
It is a condition of freedom and (some would say) moral responsibility.

Key figures
Angelina Grimké, 1805–1879
John Stuart Mill, 1806–1873
Sojourner Truth, c.1797–1883
Mary Wollstonecraft, 1759–1797

Make the connection
liberalism, p.47
intention, p.128
posthumanism, p.133

I'm free!

agency

Broadly speaking, an agent is someone or something that acts. A secret agent is someone who acts secretly, who hides their actions from others. A biological agent is a substance that acts in a certain way. We sometimes talk about 'chemical agents' in the context of warfare, referring to chemical substances, like toxins, that can be used to hurt or kill. Meanwhile, a literary agent is someone who acts on behalf of an author, and an estate agent is someone who acts on behalf of home-owners or buyers.

Clearly, not all agents are autonomous. Some agents act on behalf of other people, according to their instructions. This is true of estate agents or secret agents. If a secret agent were to act autonomously, their employer could accuse them of going rogue. They might even become a 'double agent', and act for two agencies simultaneously.

We sometimes use 'agency' and 'autonomy' interchangeably, but there are nuanced differences. While autonomy is primarily focused on the freedom and independence of individuals to make decisions (typically about themselves), agency tends to refer to the capacity of an individual to act intentionally and exert control over their environment. There is greater focus on actual action, on being an active participant in one's own life (although there are exceptions). Autonomy is typically associated with the right to choose, while agency emphasizes active individual engagement.

In a nutshell
The capacity to *act*, independently of other influences.

Why it matters
Agency overlaps with autonomy in providing a basis for moral responsibility.

Key figures
Margaret Cavendish, 1623–1673
Valerie Gray Hardcastle
Audre Lorde, 1934–1992
Mary Wollstonecraft, 1759–1797

Make the connection
liberalism, p.47
self-consciousness, p.89
autocracy, p.102

inescapability

Inescapability is one of those concepts that does pretty much exactly what it says on the tin. It appears in discussions of ethics and legal studies, where it refers to the idea that a moral principle or obligation is unavoidable and cannot be ignored, i.e., it is inescapable.

In many ethical frameworks, for instance, people are obliged to be honest. Suppose I accidentally walk out of a bookshop without paying for a book (it could happen!). I may have committed theft, but I haven't been caught. It's a small bookshop and they haven't installed any of those fancy book sensors on the doors. However, the inescapability of honesty suggests that, even though I won't suffer any negative consequences for this theft, I'm obliged to go back and pay.

The moral compulsion to be honest is inescapable. It can't be set aside or ignored. You can't avoid it by running away. Like the villains in horror films, it will always catch up with you. Inescapability emphasizes the enduring nature of moral obligations.

Of course, the possibility of escape is context-dependent, and cultures change as we reassess and re-evaluate our values. What was once inescapable might become less so. The Romans might have thought courage was an inescapable moral obligation, but other value systems might put more of a premium on kindness, deference and respect.

In a nutshell
The view that some moral obligations are unavoidable.

Why it matters
It is a central strut in much moral theory and accents our engagement with ethical dilemmas.

Key figures
Philippa Foot, 1920–2010
Christine Korsgaard, b.1952
Onora O'Neill, b.1941
Joseph Raz, 1939–2022

Make the connection

overridingness

In ethics, overridingness is the capacity of certain moral principles to take precedence over competing considerations. Unlike inescapability, which applies to specific moral values, overridingness focuses on the relation *between* obligations.

Consider a situation in which a medical doctor is trying to save a patient's life, despite the patient refusing the relevant treatment. (Maybe medical intervention runs against deeply held religious beliefs about the sinfulness of transplantation.) If the doctor continues to administer the treatment, it is because she places greater moral weight on the preservation of life than on the principle of autonomy. It isn't that she doesn't care about the patient's autonomy – their right to decide their fate for themselves – it's just that she thinks it is overridden by the need to preserve life (the 'principle of beneficence').

When a moral principle is overriding, its moral weight is considered to be greater than other principles or factors, like personal desires and preferences. Both inescapability and overridingness focus on the power of certain obligations. However, if a principle is inescapable, it cannot be overridden. This can lead to seemingly intractable moral puzzles, where one inescapable moral principle is seen to compete with another inescapable moral principle. Neither can override the other, so the moral agent (in this case) is left at an impasse.

In a nutshell
If a moral verdict is overriding, it is supposed to override other, competing verdicts.

Why it matters
Many of the puzzles in moral and ethical philosophy arise from overriding and inescapable concerns coming into conflict.

Key figures
Hannah Arendt, 1906–1975
Philippa Foot, 1920–2010
Martha Nussbaum, b.1947

Make the connection

My priority is always to save lives.

rhetoric

Have you ever wondered how words shape opinions and mould minds? Have you ever listened to great orators and wanted to possess that same strange power to persuade?

I'm not expecting you to answer these questions, by the way (or indeed any of the other questions posed in this book). They're rhetorical. That is, they're figures of speech, used not to elicit an actual response, but to engage you in what I'm writing and to make a point. A rhetorical question can give the illusion of openness and, by doing so, subtly lead you in one direction rather than another.

Rhetoric is the art of persuasion. There are many rhetorical devices, a handful of which are illustrated in the opening paragraph. Alongside rhetorical questions, there is something known as *anaphora* – repetition of a word or phrase ('have you ever . . .?') There's alliteration, which is the repetition of consonants ('mould minds', 'power to persuade'). Rhetoricians are interested in the different tools and techniques that can be used to draw audiences in.

While rhetoric was once taught alongside other philosophical subjects such as metaphysics, ethics and epistemology, it has for a long time been officially exiled from the discipline. Rhetoric is a practical art, concerned with persuading people, rather than uncovering absolute truths. As such, it is typically seen to be counter to the truth-seeking aims of philosophy.

In a nutshell
The art of persuasion.

Why it matters
Rhetoric may have been officially exiled, but academic philosophy is still heavily invested in promoting certain argumentative norms and structures.

Key figures
Margaret Cavendish, 1623–1673
Anna Julia Cooper, 1858–1964
Niccolò Machiavelli, 1469–1527
Christine de Pizan, 1364–1430

Make the connection
reasonable, p.15
irony, p.31
ideology, p.66

dialectics

While rhetoric aims to persuade, dialectics ostensibly aspires towards reasoned argument and open dialogue. The goal is not to win arguments, but to uncover underlying principles, beliefs or truths. The term comes from the Greek *dia*, meaning 'through', and *legomai*, meaning 'discourse'. Dialectics involves chatting things out, talking things through.

Most of us engage in dialectical reasoning on a daily basis. Say, for instance, that you've just asked your friend for advice on job-hunting. She wants to know what kind of work you're interested in doing. You tell her your thoughts (gherkin merchant), then ask what job she's enjoyed the most. You go back and forth like this, honing your understanding of the value of certain work, your expectations for payment, and so on. You may even disagree about the most suitable form of employment. She points out that it's very difficult to become a gherkin merchant and reminds you that you're allergic to cucumbers. You refine your expectations and between the two of you decide that a career at the pickled-egg factory is probably more reasonable.

'Dialectic' is sometimes used interchangeably with 'dialogic'. However, dialogic refers to open dialogue, while dialectic is focused on achieving a resolution. It's the difference between chatting and chatting things through in order to reach a conclusion. Both differ from rhetoric, which tends to be more one-sided and is usually used by an orator addressing an audience.

In a nutshell
A method of discourse aimed at resolving contradictions or creating a synthesis of opposing ideas.

Why it matters
This is one of the primary ways that we argue and reach agreements.

Key figures
Raya Dunayevskaya, 1910–1987
Georg Wilhelm Friedrich Hegel, 1770–1831
Alexandre Kojève, 1902–1968
Slavoj Zizek, b.1949

Make the connection
rational, p.14
analysis, p.84
semantics, p.122

Let's talk it through.

emergentism

Is a thought a physical thing? Well, not obviously. We can't touch thoughts or even see them. They are intangible. As such, they create serious problems for anyone who claims that reality is purely material, including physicalists, materialists and scientists of various stripes. If you think the only stuff that exists is physical, you will have some difficulty explaining the existence of thoughts.

One way around this problem is 'emergentism'. For the emergentist, thoughts and consciousness in general are 'emergent properties' of physical things like brains. When you have particles arranged into complex neurological systems, new properties can 'emerge'. These properties aren't simply combinations of the properties of the particles – they're not *reducible* to them. But they're dependent on them. If the material stuff is absent, the emergent properties are absent too.

Think about the way wetness emerges as a property of water. Water is composed of hydrogen and oxygen particles, which aren't themselves wet. But when you have a sufficient number of them together, you get a new property: wetness. It's not reducible, but it's dependent on the particular stuff. Or imagine a flower market. On one level, it's just a collection of people erecting stalls next to each other and selling flowers. But a sufficiently complex arrangement can lead to emergent properties – the flower market may become a tourist attraction. This property isn't reducible to the constituent parts, but is dependent upon them.

In a nutshell
The view that mental properties can depend on physical properties and processes without being reducible to them.

Why it matters
This is one way we can acknowledge the specialness of consciousness without arguing for immaterial substances.

Key figures
John Dupré, b.1952
Jerome A. Shaffer, 1929–2002
A. N. Whitehead, 1861–1947

Make the connection
qualitative identity, p.58
materialism, p.124
particle theory, p.140

This is more than just a bunch of flowers!

epiphenomenalism

The epiphenomenalists hold that seemingly higher-level phenomena, such as consciousness and mental states, are by-products of physical processes and have no causal impact on physical events. We might be able to describe a flower market as a tourist attraction, but on an explanatory level we are simply talking about a bunch of flower stalls grouped together.

For the epiphenomenalist, consciousness and conscious experiences are simply the mental by-product of physical processes. We may think we're influencing physical events (I have the distinct feeling that my thoughts are prompting me to type out these sentences), but such thoughts are causally inert. Neurons are firing, producing specific, predictable effects, and my experience is simply the *observation* of the causal chain. Despite my assumptions to the contrary, my thoughts aren't linked up to my actions.

Both emergentism and epiphenomenalism attempt to explain seemingly non-physical events without violating physicalism, the thesis that everything can be explained through reference to physical things and the forces that hold them together. Both are distinct from dualism, the view that there's physical stuff (the subject of physics), but also other, immaterial stuff, like souls. However, of the two, the emergentist is more hopeful, believing (for instance) that mental phenomena can exert causal effects on physical processes. The epiphenomenalist denies any causal influence of mental properties.

In a nutshell
The view that mental states are caused by physical states but don't cause anything themselves.

Why it matters
Ardent epiphenomenalists will deny that our conscious experience of the world has any impact on what we end up doing.

Key figures
Thomas Huxley, 1825–1895
Frank Jackson, 1943–2020
Baruch Spinoza, 1632–1677

Make the connection
consciousness, p.88
physicalism, p.125
indeterminism, p.130

I'm thinking but not doing.

'philosophy'

The word 'philosophy' is Greek in origin. It is derived from *philo*, which means 'love', and *sophia*, which means 'wisdom'. Philosophy is the love of wisdom.

In higher education, philosophy is normally framed as a single, discrete discipline. It is formed of various subdisciplines, including epistemology, metaphysics, aesthetics and ethics (which are themselves made up of sub-subdisciplines such as meta-ethics and meta-metaphysics).

However these disciplinary categories are relatively recent innovations. Once upon a time, not that long ago in fact, 'philosophy' referred to something more like a super-discipline. It included pretty much everything, from politics, rhetoric and economics to medical science, chemistry and physics. The term 'natural philosopher' referred to people we would nowadays think of as scientists.

Given this history, it's not entirely clear what the words 'philosophy' and 'philosophical' actually refer to. Consequently, some people suggest that 'philosophical' refers less to the topics and more to ways of approaching discussions. In this broader sense, physicists and medical doctors can be just as philosophical as philosophers. Some readers may object to the people I have identified as philosophers in this book (there is always controversy about who is and isn't part of a group), but when the disciplinary boundaries are vague, I think it is better to err on the side of being generous than not.

In a nutshell
A seemingly discrete academic discipline, with boundaries much vaguer than we might at first assume.

Why it matters
Including or excluding different topics from a discipline can affect whether or not they appear to be legitimate areas of inquiry.

Key figures
Peter Adamson, b.1972
Yoko Arisaka, b.1962
Chris Meyns

Make the connection
poststructuralism, p.11
ideology, p.66
hermeneutics, p.123

philosophy

It is relevant that so much of this book is focused on etymology (from the Greek *etumon*, meaning 'meaning', and *logia*, meaning 'study'). It is also relevant that so many of the terms discussed are Greek and Latin in origin. In the Anglophone sphere, 'philosophy' usually, implicitly, refers to a tradition of thought that has its origins in the culture of Ancient Greece and Rome. The same is true in most Euro-American academic environments and, indeed, in countries whose education systems are the result of European and American colonial expansion.

Mainstream philosophy tends to be true to its etymological roots. It privileges the interests of the Hellenic tradition and the schools of thought that emerged from it (Christianity, for instance). As a result, it also excludes other traditions of thought, which – if there were a more expansive conception of philosophy – we would see are equally loving of wisdom.

It is only in recent years that mainstream Western philosophy has begun to open its borders and admit what Anglophone philosophers occasional refer to (patronizingly) as 'World Philosophy' or 'Global Philosophy'. This includes Africana, Islamic, Native American and Indian traditions of thought, which are every bit as rich – and often much older – than the Hellenic philosophical tradition in which I was trained. Whether the discipline can adapt to become more representative and inclusive is an important – and open – question.

In a nutshell
Western conceptions of philosophy privilege the Hellenic tradition.

Why it matters
This is only a partial picture of philosophical engagement, privileging certain voices over others.

Key figures
Lewis Gordon, b.1962
Kwame Nkrumah, 1909–1972
Ngũgĩ wa Thiong'o, b.1938

Make the connection
power, p.41
domination, p.53
hegemony, p.67

movers & shakers

The following, highly selective list highlights 20 key figures currently working in the field of philosophy. These are the 'movers and shakers' reshaping this millennia-old discipline.

Sara Ahmed is a scholar-activist engaged in institutional critique. What does it feel like to be a person of colour working in white systems? What are the affective effects of certain official, formal spaces on marginalised groups? Using her own experience, and first-hand testimony, Ahmed documents the experience of coming up against institutional power.

Linda Martín Alcoff is an epistemologist who specializes in social epistemology, philosophy of race and decolonial theory. She is interested in the effects of prejudice on what we know, and how we come to know it. If you are prejudiced against a specific group, you may give them less credibility. They will be given less 'epistemic respect', a 'credibility deficit'.

Elizabeth Anderson (b.1959) is an American political theorist with an interest in affirmative action. In *The Imperative of Integration* (2010), Anderson argues that diversity for its own sake is insufficient, and that social institutions need to actively integrate marginalized groups, while simultaneously dismantling structural barriers to access.

Moya Bailey is an American scholar credited with coining the term 'misogynoir', which addresses the intersection of racism and misogyny experienced by Black women. Bailey's work involves a critical examination of the ways that popular culture perpetuates harmful stereotypes and marginalizes Black women.

Nora Berenstain is an epistemologist who looks at how conversational conventions (such as 'being polite') can affect what we know and how. Her concept of 'epistemic exploitation' addresses some of the downsides to asking well-meaning questions of marginalised groups.

Talia Mae Bettcher is a scholar-activist perhaps best known for their work on gender and transgender identity. Reflecting on their own experience of transition, they have articulated the socio-cultural and political pressures experienced by many trans folk.

Darren Chetty (b.1972) has been, in recent years, one of reasonableness's most ardent critics. Writing in the British context, where politicians often invoke 'reasonable' or 'commonsensical' behaviour, he draws out the extent to which such appeals rely on behavioural norms of politesse, good manners and social niceties.

Patricia Hill Collins (b.1948) is a sociologist and social epistemologist. In *Black Feminist Thought* (1990), she describes a standpoint epistemology, which acknowledges the additional insights to which people of colour have access, by virtue of living in a racist society, and knowing how to resist it.

Kimberlé Crenshaw (b.1959) is a legal scholar, critical race theorist and civil rights advocate. In her 1989 essay 'Demarginalizing the Intersection of Race and Sex', she introduced the concept of intersectionality into mainstream discourse.

Kristie Dotson (b.1975) is an American social epistemologist, whose work explores how bodies of knowledge (like those held in university libraries) are accented in specific and often exclusionary ways. What are the standards by which we assess whether a belief is justified, and do these standards favour some groups? Dotson argues that maybe, yes, they do.

Judith Jack Halberstam (b.1961) is an American academic and author who has made significant contributions to the fields of gender and queer studies. They encourage us to understand biological sex as a spectrum of possibilities rather than a simple binary, and advocate for a more inclusive understanding of individuals.

Donna Haraway (b.1944) is a cultural theorist and historian of science, whose work explores the interconnections between technology, gender and identity. Her 'Cyborg Manifesto' questions the traditional boundaries between organic and non-organic, between nature and culture.

Linda Hogan (b.1947) is a Chickasaw poet, essayist and environmentalist, recognised for her work on the intersections of indigenous spirituality, environmentalism and social justice. Her 1994 novel *Solar Storms* is informed by Native American spiritual traditions, intertwining animism with environmentalist themes

Zeus Leonardo draws insights from sociology, academic philosophy and cultural studies to inform his analysis of the relationship between schooling, the structure of academic institutions and race, class, culture and gender. Working in the United States, he is often positioned within the Critical Race Theory (CRT) movement, though he resists this framing.

Sabina Lovibond is a British ethicist who has written extensively about the role of emotions in moral psychology, examining how they shape our ethical judgements and decision-making. Unlike the rationalists, she examines how emotions contribute (sometimes positively) to our perceptions of moral situations.

Kate Manne (b.1983), in her 2018 book *Down Girl*, uses 'sexism' to refer to a system of beliefs and practices that enforce patriarchal norms and gender hierarchies. In contrast to sexism, she describes 'misogyny' as both the hatred of women and as a social force that punishes women who deviate from traditional gender roles.

José Medina is interested in the degree to which we are open to challenges and new ways of thinking. In books like *The Epistemology of Resistance* (2012), he examines how we close ourselves off from critique and protect ourselves from alternative ways of being in the world. He suggests that radical open-mindedness is necessary for social and political change.

Uma Narayan is a feminist scholar whose work critically engages with the Western philosophical tradition and its literary canon. She has been heavily critical of universalist approaches that import Western moral frameworks into cultural contexts that recognise different, possibly conflicting values and practices.

Susan Oyama (b.1943) is a psychologist and philosopher of science whose work has focused on, among other things, the 'nature–nurture' debate. In *Evolution's Eye* (2000), she examines how genetics and environmental factors affect human development. She criticizes the view that genes alone determine the characteristics of an organism.

Shirley Anne Tate (b.1956) is a sociologist whose work focuses on the Black diaspora, mixed race studies and feminism. Her research into normative beauty standards examines the politics of visibility within Black anti-racist aesthetics. What is seen? What is not seen? What is celebrated, what is not celebrated?

Calvin L. Warren is an American scholar and a contributor to the field of 'Black Nihilism', itself related to 'Afro-pessimism'. Both areas engage with the sense of hopelessness brought about within white supremacy. Warren explores the limits and dangers of hope and enriches existentialist thought, which has historically neglected Black experiences.

index

IVY PRESS

**First published in 2025 by Ivy Press
an imprint of The Quarto Group.**

One Triptych Place, London, SE1 9SH, United Kingdom
T (0)20 7700 6700
www.Quarto.com

A catalogue record for this book is available from the British Library.

ISBN 978-0-71129-887-3
Ebook ISBN 978-0-71129-888-0

Design by Intercity
Editor Faye Robson
Production Manager Rohana Yusof
Series Editor Jane Wilsher
We would like to extend our thanks to Guntaas Kaur
Chugh for providing an inclusivity read on the book.

Printed in China
10 9 8 7 6 5 4 3 2 1